RESPONSIVE LITERACY COACHING

Tools for Creating and Sustaining Purposeful Change

Cheryl Dozier

FOREWORD BY PETER H. JOHNSTON

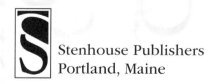

Stenhouse Publishers
Portland, Maine

Stenhouse Publishers
www.stenhouse.com

Copyright © 2006 by Cheryl Dozier

Every effort has been made to contact copyright holders and students for permission to reproduce borrowed material. We regret any oversights that may have occurred and will be pleased to rectify them in subsequent reprints of the work.

Library of Congress Cataloging-in-Publication Data
Dozier, Cheryl.
    Responsive literacy coaching : tools for creating and sustaining
    purposeful change / Cheryl Dozier.
       p. cm.
    Includes bibliographical references and index.
    ISBN-13: 978-1-57110-463-2
    ISBN-10: 1-57110-463-1
    1. Language arts teachers--Training of. 2. Language arts. I. Title.

LB2844.1.R4D69 2006
372.6044--dc22

                                        2006050479

Cover design, interior design, and typesetting by
studio 7 design

Manufactured in the United States of America on acid-free paper
12 11   9 8 7 6 5 4 3

In memory of
Carol Lilly Bond
my mother
my coach

Contents

Foreword

These are trying times for teachers. We know more than we ever have about teaching, learning, and literacy and their complexities. Yet we persist with public policies that assume that if we just increase the pressure on teachers to improve their students' test scores, they will somehow teach better— and perhaps faster—and that children will develop literacies that will engage them and carry them into the future. We persist with administrative strategies based on the assumption that teaching can best be improved by simply having experts write scripted programs for teachers to follow, regardless of the characteristics of the children in their classes. Neither approach is supported by evidence.

Teaching cannot be improved by simply opening a canned "whoop-ass teaching" program, nor can it be improved by punishing teachers whose students do not perform as we imagine they should. In the face of these institutional and administrative pressures, many school districts and professional organizations have looked to coaching as a more sane way to help teachers and schools build the institutional and individual learning required to move children and education forward. This book, engagingly and accessibly written, offers the conceptual and practical tools needed to coach teachers effectively. If we make the shift to coaching and coaches are not well prepared, we will repeat our history of "tried that—didn't work."

Coaching is not easy. There are many pitfalls (and I am personally acquainted with most of them). Coaches easily can appear to teachers as if they were saying, "We're from the government. We're here to help you." Making changes in one's teaching can seem very risky, particularly when your students' test scores will become public knowledge. It can be hard to look unflinchingly at your own teaching. Sometimes, the more you care about your students the harder it is to face the need to change. Changing one's practice can seem to imply that your previous practices had negative consequences for your students. It can be difficult for an experienced teacher to confront the fact that years of well-praised teaching may no longer meet students' needs in a changing world. Sometimes teachers are divided into factions, each of which presumes to have the right approach and waits for you, the coach, to choose sides. Cheryl addresses complexities and pitfalls like these with clarity.

Cheryl's book is not simply aimed at improving teaching through coaching. She teaches us that improving teaching means helping teachers become responsive to their students' knowledge, goals, interests, experiences, and practices. It means taking students from where they are to where they can go while leaving the students in control of their learning. To get responsive teaching, coaches need what Cheryl calls responsive coaching. Responsive coaching requires the development of an eye for what to notice in teachers; an active, yet patient ear for learning where they are coming from; and a tongue that is not hasty and carries a language of growth, reflection, and agency. Teaching doesn't improve by force. It improves as teachers come to understand what they are doing, why they are doing it, and with whom they are doing it. They need to know what their options are, and need a community of colleagues who support their problem-solving and encourage them to challenge themselves. Responsive coaching helps teachers capitalize on their own literacy and learning experiences without becoming trapped in them. It creates social spaces in which teachers can feel safe sharing half-baked possibilities, analyzing errors, and seeking and examining evidence while keeping their heads up and their eyes on the big picture—educating resilient children for an advanced and rapidly changing democracy.

Coaching is a big responsibility and the expectations are high, but coaching strategies have been obscure until now. Classroom experience by itself does not prepare us for coaching. I have encountered several teachers who, having been recognized for their teaching, were recruited into full-time coaching positions only to face hurdles they could not have imagined and return to their classrooms defeated. If only this book were available to them! I have encountered young and enthusiastic teachers who have been recruited into coaching only to be rebuffed as "upstarts." The field has desperately needed a book that helps coaches take teachers from where they are to where they might be and that shows how to build the learning communities necessary to sustain people through the stresses and joys of learning and change.

I have admired Cheryl as a teacher and as a teacher of teachers for a number of years now, and with this book my admiration continues to grow. Two years ago, looking to improve my own teaching, I spent time watching Cheryl teach. Through this engaging book you will come to know Cheryl Dozier as a gifted teacher of children and of their teachers. In fact, she is a gifted teacher of learners of all ages, even ones who would prefer not to learn just now, thank you very much. The book is practical, theoretically coherent, and engagingly written. It is filled with detailed coaching strategies, including extensive dialogue from interactions with teachers and students. The book maintains seamless parallels between teaching children and coaching teachers, weaving in children's literature along the way. It offers straightforward strategies for effective coaching, but it also offers a framework, a way of thinking which by itself would move you towards coaching strategically. Cheryl shows us that neither coaching nor teaching is a matter of simply delivering knowledge to people. She helps us to remember that it is not about becoming a good teacher or being "exemplary." It is about constantly improving our practice, and constantly striving for our students' optimal and self-extending learning. In any teaching it matters what we say, and Cheryl offers us many specific examples of interactions. One of my favorites is when, having come up with a strategy, Cheryl asks, "How many ways could this go wrong?" She then asks how these potential pitfalls might be handled. One of the beauties of Cheryl's coaching is that she doesn't pretend that instructional strategies always work. Quite the reverse. This practice of thinking through possibilities and performing mental experiments ensures that teachers don't get trapped and paralyzed in instructional dead ends. At the same time, it pulls skeptics and naysayers into the conversation and neutralizes negativity by involving them in productive problem-solving.

This book answers the question, "How does a coach create the necessary learning space for experienced and inexperienced teachers alike to expand their zones of proximal development and to take the risks necessary for their teaching to grow?" This book is firmly grounded in several forms of research on children's and teachers' learning, not the least of which is Cheryl's own work (e.g., Dozier 2001; Dozier, Johnston, and Rogers 2006; Dozier and Rutten 2005/2006). And yet it has a personal, even intimate feel to it, particularly because she also draws heavily on her history of successful teaching and coaching. This is an extremely important and timely book. It offers a rich and detailed vision of coaching, teaching, learning, and literacy. If you coach, mentor, have a teacher study group, are a principal, or work with teachers in any way, this book will help you improve teaching.

Peter H. Johnston

Acknowledgments

I am surrounded by extraordinary friends and colleagues. This community supports and extends my thinking, my knowing, and my being. Every person offers a unique strength, and this book is stronger because each is central to my life.

Susan Garnett and I have researched together, taught together, and learned together. Susan read countless drafts with meticulous care, and her gentle voice, ever-present optimism, and careful crafting guided and inspired me. While writing this book, our friendship became a steadying presence in my life. Linda Shekita nudged when I needed a nudge, celebrated when I needed to sit back and savor, and helped me rethink when I lost my way, as only a best friend can. The conversations behind this book and my work started more than fifteen years ago as Linda and I sat in my infant daughter Kate's room raising questions about teacher development, change, and the language we use as educators.

Becky Rogers is fearless as a writer and encourages me, always, to write from my soul. Vanessa LaRae was encouraging and envisioned identities I was not yet ready to consider.

I have had the good fortune to work with several administrators who believe in responsive coaching and know that empowering teachers matters for children and their families. I am grateful to the many teachers I work with who trusted and welcomed me into their classrooms and into their worlds. Our shared experiences are at the core of this book. I am indebted to the teachers who wrote vignettes and brought their classroom experiences to life.

The Dr. Nuala McGann Drescher Affirmative Action/ Diversity Leave Program through the University at Albany and the United University Profession provided time to write this book. I am also grateful for the encouragement and support of my colleagues at the University at Albany, Stephanie Affinito, Heidi Andrade, Jim Collins, Ginny Goatley, Abbe Herzig, Peter Johnston, Mark Jury, George Kamberelis, Donna Scanlon, Miriam Raider-Roth, Carol Rodgers, Margi Sheehy, Sean Walmsley, Trudy Walp, and RoseMarie Weber. Mary Unser and Linda Papa provide a cheerful and calming presence on a daily basis. Ginny Goatley provided constructive and valuable suggestions to drafts and chapters as I explored ideas and articulated issues. In South Africa Ginny helped clarify my thinking on sustaining change. Peter Johnston has been a mentor, friend, and colleague. I appreciate his generous and thought-provoking foreword to this book. Peter's words and thoughts continue to push me to think more deeply. I am a better writer, thinker, teacher, and learner because of his valuable insights and thoughtful critiques.

My editor, Bill Varner, engaged in his own responsive coaching throughout this project. Bill offered perfectly timed questions to drafts, moved the project forward with humor and understanding, and provided space for me to heal and grieve when my mother died. I am grateful to Philippa Stratton for taking on this project and to Erin Whitehead and Jay Kilburn for their assistance and feedback in bringing the book to publication. The insightful and thoughtful critiques by an anonymous reviewer expanded my thinking throughout the process of writing this book.

Most important, I am grateful for my family. My children, Kate, Michael, and Nicholas, continue to teach me the importance of being responsive and are constant sources of inspiration. My husband, Joseph Chiseri, provides unwavering support, patience, and love. My mother, Carol Lilly Bond, a teacher for thirty-two years, died while I was writing this book. Her joy and interest in my teaching and writing were ever present. In ways most important, she remained with me to the conclusion of this book. I will forever remember the sparkle in her blue eyes and the smile on her face as we talked about this book during our last lunch together at York Beach.

Introduction

For me, life is about connections and connectedness.
Teaching is about connections and connectedness.
Responsive literacy coaching is about connections and
connectedness. How do we find points of connectedness
as we learn together, support one another, and collaborate?
How do we come to understand a learner's zone of proximal
development? How do we awaken possibilities, recognize
fears, and set the table for successful learning experiences
and opportunities? What do we do to engender trust, to
maintain sensitivity, to find a balance between supporter and
"nudger," to listen carefully, to be empathetic, to step in and
step out of lives—teachers' lives and children's lives?

In this book I draw from twenty-four years of teaching
experience working side by side with teachers and students
in multiple roles and contexts. These educational settings
include urban schools, suburban schools, and a university
literacy lab. Moving between and among these spaces,

I am reminded daily how challenging it is to be a learner. I have worked with learners from kindergarten through the doctoral level—learners who took risks and were fearless, learners who wanted to be perfect and not make a mistake, and learners who were unsure whether learning was an enterprise for them to engage in.

My first teaching position was a "split" kindergarten in two schools several miles apart in an urban district. Each day I traveled between buildings in my royal blue Pinto with crates filled with paints, glue, glitter, markers, construction paper, a hot plate for cooking, record albums, and read-alouds. We sang, we painted, we read, we cooked, and we went on walking field trips through the city. The next year I taught second grade. One building. One classroom. I was thrilled. Now I had an anchor. My students fell in love with biographies, and so did I. They taught me to love writing. After several years of teaching second grade, I moved to a newly opened humanities magnet school, where I taught third grade and collaborated with the librarian, music teacher, and art teacher to develop inquiry projects. I brought my grandmother's rocking chair into my classroom for read-alouds, and we began the year observing the metamorphosis of four monarch butterflies. The room was huge and filled with student work, models of Mount Olympus, animal research reports with clay figures, hanging planet mobiles, and a class book written after researching famous Americans. I still remember Adam walking up to me one day and asking, "Why don't we study white men?"

My principal encouraged me to become an administrator. I took one course, received an A, and concluded I was not meant to be an administrator. Even though I was ready to try something new, I needed to remain closer to the classroom. I applied for a newly created position to work with ten school districts as a literacy staff developer. In this position I worked in the districts as they redesigned their literacy programs—developing workshops, modeling lessons in more than 100 classrooms, presenting at parent nights, and providing guidance for administrators. The districts were vastly different in terms of funding, emphasis on professional development, materials, and expectations of students and teachers.

Now, as a teacher educator at a university, I continue to work closely in and with school districts. Each context informs the other and becomes inextricably woven. My classroom experiences provide a grounding for preparing future literacy teachers. At the university literacy lab I have the best of both worlds: teaching children *and* teaching teachers. Together, we engage in a range of responsive instructional practices and examine theories, all the while remaining connected to children, teaching, and learning.

No learning situation is ever the same. Each moment brings its own complexities, its own intricacies, its own spaces for coming to know. I still travel with crates in my minivan. Now my crates are filled with mentor texts, professional readings, my writer's notebook, models for family literacy journals, and examples of interesting children's writing. Markers and engaging read-alouds will always remain a mainstay.

Literacy coaching is currently a hot topic in education and is considered a "powerful intervention with great potential" (International Reading Association 2004) to increase student literacy achievement. At national, state, and local levels coaching is being touted as a way to improve reading instruction and increase student achievement. In this book, I argue that at its best, literacy coaching is responsive, collegial, thoughtful, thought-provoking, deliberate, reflective, and transferable. To achieve this, literacy coaches develop and extend their in-depth content knowledge, leadership capabilities, and flexibility and competence as they navigate the range of roles and responsibilities they encounter in their instructional contexts.

With competing calls for teacher proof materials and scripted programs (Allington 2002), this book instead provides a framework for thinking about responsive literacy coaching and responsive teaching that honors teachers and learners and their developing understandings. As assessment scores are scrutinized, literacy tasks documented and analyzed, and coaching interactions logged and categorized, we must remain mindful to avoid being so caught up "in the doing" of coaching that we forget the *purpose* of what we are doing. This book invites you to step back, pause, and ask, What is our goal? What is our purpose? What type of literacy environments and experiences are we creating in our schools for our students?

My goal in this book is to offer a range of tools that will empower responsive coaches and teachers through conversation and dialogue, sustained engagement, and reflective analysis. The instructional tools foster teachers' critical thinking and reflection so that they, in turn, support their students to think critically. These tools are designed to create environments where continuous change is expected while also acknowledging tensions and difficulties inherent in the change process. The tools promote reflection as teachers consider plausible and possible instructional practices. As such, the tools are guideposts, not absolutes. Although using the tools will not provide a "quick fix" (Allington and Walmsley 1995), it will lead to sustained inquiry. It is hard work, especially given that prescribed lessons and prepackaged materials are readily available, making it easy to fall into unexamined or "it's always been done this way" practices. Literacy teaching is more than a compilation of interesting and engaging "best practices" (Anders, Hoffman, and Duffy 2000, 719).

Rethinking instructional practices can be unnerving. It is far easier to ignore the complexities of learning and the attending uncomfortable moments that accompany being out of our "safe" zones. As responsive literacy coaches, it is our job to be mindful of our learners—teachers—and support them and ourselves to take risks as they and we engage in new instructional practices. As coaches, how do we support and foster the hard work of examining learning and teaching?

How do we take (and encourage our teachers to take) an agentive stance and take responsibility for pedagogical decisions and instructional practices and their effect? Not all teachers embrace change from the outset. Some prefer to "toe in," some dive in, and others remain on the side, not yet ready to enter the water. As coaches, we learn from everyone.

It is my hope that this book will support you in your development as a responsive literacy coach and simultaneously provide teaching and learning tools for the teachers you are coaching. The vignettes and examples woven throughout bring together multiple voices from teachers, coaches, administrators, and students from a range of classrooms and school districts. (All student names are pseudonyms.) This multiplicity of voices is intentional and seeks to complicate our collective thinking about teaching, learning, and literacy coaching. Although each vignette speaks to the particulars of a classroom, a district, and a teaching context, it also raises issues for considering the universals of classrooms. As you read, consider what suggestions and ideas could be transferred to your particular context and which would need alterations (sometimes minor and sometimes more extensive) for your coaching context.

The way each teacher views literacy and literacy instruction is unique. Each classroom is unique. Each building is unique. Each school district is unique. Each interaction brings an opportunity for reexamination and further exploration. It is my hope that this book invites you to discuss, to wonder anew, to welcome the challenge and excitement of working with teachers and children.

Welcome!

01 What Is Responsive Literacy Coaching?

Taped on my wall at work is the saying, "Lucky is the woman who has found her true work." My wall also includes a picture of my daughter holding a koala bear, a greeting card with hairy legs and the phrase "bad hair day," a New Yorker calendar, photos of my family in New York City, a panoramic view of the Grand Canyon, and several pictures of the ocean at York, Maine. My desk includes chocolates (always!), lavender hand cream, and a feng shui box with a rake, stones, and beach sand. On my writing desk at home, I have a photo of a sunset taken by my mother, a sculpture of a family of five from South Africa, an angel given to me by my aunt as I cared for my dying mother, and a clock with the saying "No time like the present." My desks are also filled with books—novels, short stories, poetry, children's books, professional books. I look to these artifacts for strength, for sustenance, for inspiration. The artifacts on my desks and in my working spaces invite conversation; they invite connectedness. They invite people to participate. They are some of the tools I use to help me as I wonder anew and consider what it means to be a teacher, a coach, a learner.

With increased national attention on improving student literacy achievement, reading is the focus of initiatives at both the state and federal levels. Some states have targeted federal dollars to fund reading coaches to improve reading instruction. According to the International Reading Association, "a rapid proliferation of reading coaches is one of the responses to increased attention to reading achievement and the achievement gap in the United States" (2004, 1). By engaging in local professional development, literacy coaches help teachers learn about reading processes and become more expert at teaching reading. Lyons (2002) maintains that informed one-on-one coaching based on students' behaviors improves teachers' knowledge base, analytic skills, and expertise.

The International Reading Association (2004) identifies five criteria that literacy coaching must meet to achieve its potential. Coaches must first be excellent classroom teachers and teachers of reading. Second, they must be able to observe, model in classrooms, and provide feedback to teachers. Third, they must be knowledgeable about reading processes, acquisition, assessment, and instruction. Fourth, they must have experience working with teachers to improve instructional practices. And in this capacity, fifth, they must be excellent presenters and be able to lead teacher groups to facilitate reflection and change. Because a coach plays a central role in professional development, the International Reading Association also identified essential features for effective professional development. Professional development should be "grounded in inquiry and reflection, participant-driven and collaborative, involving a sharing of knowledge among teachers within communities of practice, sustained, ongoing, and intensive, and connected to and derived from teachers ongoing work with their students" (2006, 3). Literacy coaches work primarily with teachers, but for reform efforts to be successful, they must also engage the broader educational community, including administrators, students, and families.

The model for literacy coaching presented in this book encompasses both the criteria for literacy coaching and the essential features of professional development outlined by the IRA. Within a trusting and collaborative learning community, teachers grow, question, wonder, and learn to trust themselves as professionals and as learners. Teachers come to view themselves as public intellectuals (Commeyras 2002). To question what changes are necessary to support teachers and learners in their particular contexts, literacy coaches invite collaborative intellectual inquiry. As co-learners (Cambourne 1995), literacy coaches engage in the change process as knowledgeable others, rather than as experts. Although coaches do not assume the role of expert, it is important for them to draw from and acknowledge areas of expertise, just as teachers do when they support students' literacy development. For coaching to make a difference, teachers must transfer their understandings and pedagogical practices from the coaching environment to their classroom practices.

As you read this book and I write this book, we each bring our collective teaching experiences and theoretical constructs to the table. My theoretical framing for responsive literacy coaching draws from and synthesizes earlier research (Dozier 2001; Dozier, Johnston, and Rogers 2006; Dozier and Rutten 2005/2006; Tharp and Gallimore 1988). At the core of responsive literacy coaching is developing respectful, caring instructional relationships. Although each of the following components of responsive literacy coaching is explored in future chapters, here is an overview of the theoretical framing. Responsive literacy coaching relationships are built on the following:

- understanding how teachers and children learn by locating the learners' zones of proximal development

(ZPD) (Vygotsky 1978) and confronting learning histories (Cole and Knowles 2000);

- structuring and engaging in "joint productive activities" (Tharp and Gallimore 1988) where coaches, teachers, and children interact to construct and co-construct knowledge;

- examining language to consider the effect and consequences of our language choices (Delpit 2002; Johnston 2004; Mercer 2000);

- building self-extending systems (Clay 1991; 2001) of understandings and strategies to generate further learning (Lyons, Pinnell, and DeFord 1993) as literacy teachers/educators.

Using this theoretical frame, this book offers parallel goals for coaches to engage teachers and for teachers, in turn, to engage students. Throughout the book, the parallel nature of coaching and teaching are made explicit. When teachers engage in a dynamic professional development process and develop practices and competencies for increased student achievement, this, in turn, becomes a model for teachers to create classroom environments where students are responsible for their learning. As teachers transfer content knowledge and practices from their coaching experiences, they build on their self-extending systems, just as they guide students in their classrooms to do the same.

It is important to note that although literacy coaches work primarily with teachers, all coaching work is situated. Coaches also engage with students, administrators, and families. Teachers teach students, collaborate with other teachers, and engage with families and administrators. Responsive literacy coaches bring together multiple participants to engage in a collaborative and collective inquiry around instructional practices and literacy learning. Table 1–1 illustrates the multiple layers of learning in coaching and teaching collaborations.

Table 1–1. Parallel Learning Goals for Responsive Literacy Coaching
Coaches: Teachers, Teachers: Students

THEORETICAL FRAMING	COACHES ↔ TEACHERS	TEACHERS ↔ STUDENTS
BUILDING OF RELATIONSHIPS Noddings 1984, 2005; Raider-Roth 2005	Develop respectful, caring instructional relationships Coaches to teachers Teachers to coaches Teachers to teachers Coaches to students* Coaches to administrators* Coaches-teachers-families*	Develop respectful, caring instructional relationships Teachers to students Teachers to teachers Students to teachers* Teachers-students-families* Families-students-teachers* Teachers-administrators-teachers*
UNDERSTANDING LEARNING Cole and Knowles 2000; Darling-Hammond and McLaughlin 1996; Gallimore and Tharp 1990; Purcell-Gates 1995; Vinz 1996; Vygotsky 1978	Understand how teachers and children learn · Recognize and examine/confront learning histories · Find learners' zones of proximal development	Understand how children learn · Value/honor learning histories · Find learners' zones of proximal development
ENGAGING IN JOINT PRODUCTIVE ACTIVITIES Lave and Wenger 1991; Tharp et al. 2000; Tharp and Gallimore 1988	Structure and engage in joint productive activities in teacher's zone to construct and co-construct knowledge	Structure and engage in joint productive activities in student's zone to construct and co-construct knowledge
LANGUAGE CHOICES Delpit 2002; Johnston 2004; Lyons, Pinnell, and DeFord 1993: Mercer 2000	Examine language choices · Articulate literacy, literacy development, and strategic knowing · Theorize while engaging in collaborative inquiry	Examine language choices · Articulate strategic knowing · Engage in collaborative inquiry
BUILD SELF-EXTENDING SYSTEMS Clay 1991, 2001; Dozier, Johnston, and Rogers 2006; Dozier and Rutten 2005/2006; Lyons, Pinnell, and DeFord 1993	Develop self-extending system · Construct and co-construct knowledge · Transfer · Problem-posing/problem-solving · Social justice · Leadership/change agent	Develop self-extending system · Construct and co-construct knowledge · Transfer · Problem-posing/problem-solving · Social justice · Activism

Table 1–2 identifies the tools in the text, provides a brief explanation, articulates the purpose of each tool, and then locates the theoretical framing behind each one. You will find that some of the tools are more conceptual in nature, whereas others are more practically oriented. Because no coaching relationship is the same, coaches, like teachers, draw from a repertoire of tools to best meet the needs of their learners. Some of the tools are readily implemented,

Table 1–2: Tools for Responsive Literacy Coaching

TOOL	EXPLANATION	PURPOSE	THEORETICAL FRAMING
Engage in Literacy Events (Chapter 2)	Examine range of ways teachers navigate expectations and demands of the literacy event.	Locate learners' zones of proximal development (ZPD). Identify needs as learners. Consider implications for classroom.	Understand how children and teachers learn.
Sharing Our Literate Lives (Chapter 2)	Explore and examine personal literacy histories.	Make known the beliefs and theories that influence your teaching.	Understand how children and teachers learn.
Team-Teach Lessons (Chapter 3)	Extend and refine instructional practices.	Consider multiple pedagogical possibilities. Become astute observers of children's literacy development.	Engage in joint productive activities.
Examine Student Work (Chapter 3)	Focus on child's strengths and needs. Analyze details of the student's work.	Ground conversations in the work of the child. Theorize about different forms of evidence. Consider student strengths in different instructional contexts.	Engage in joint productive activities.
Communicating with Others (Chapter 4)	Build learning communities and invite participation.	Consider the effect and consequences our language choices have on others.	Examine language.
Selecting and Sharing Texts (Chapter 4)	Examine text selections, from professional readings for teachers, to text choices in classrooms for students.	Consider the effect and consequences our text selections have on learners.	Examine language.
Naming Our Literate Work|Processes|Strategies (Chapter 4)	Name craft/text features, reading processes, and strategies used. Notice and identify literacy development.	Understand literate behaviors and literacy development. Develop a shared language among participants.	Examine language.
Sharing and Naming Celebrations (Chapter 4)	Articulate the range of ways teachers are extending/ refining/developing instructional practices, and identify students' growth and development.	Reframe the way we think about teaching and learning. Avoid deficit-driven theorizing.	Examine language.
Study Groups (Chapter 5)	Develop study groups and teacher research groups based upon teachers' interests.	Create and extend learning communities.	Build self-extending systems.
Transcribing Lessons and Conferring with Teachers (Chapter 5)	Analyze teaching/instructional practices through predictable framework.	Extend teaching and learning possibilities.	Build self-extending systems.
Visiting Colleagues' Classrooms (Chapter 5)	Visit classrooms to collaborate and confer with colleagues.	Generate conversations and inquiry around teaching and learning.	Build self-extending systems.
Extending the Learning Community: Sharing Knowledge (Chapter 5)	Present at conferences, workshops. Write articles for journals.	Share insights gained with others. Extend learning community.	Build self-extending systems.

"on the go" so to speak, whereas others develop over time, as relationships evolve. Some of the tools are designed primarily for one-on-one interactions, and others work for grade-level meetings or larger group sessions. All the tools are intended for working with and learning from teachers. As you read the chart, find your entry point for responsive coaching and where you would like to begin.

BUILDING RESPECTFUL, CARING INSTRUCTIONAL RELATIONSHIPS

Developing relationships is at the heart of responsive teaching. It is also at the heart of responsive literacy coaching. Responsive literacy coaches honor and respect teachers' knowledge, expertise, and understandings and seek to affirm, extend, and refine teachers' instructional practices. Noddings, in addressing the importance of relationships in learning, notes, "The caring teacher strives first to establish and maintain caring relations, and these relations exhibit an integrity that provides a foundation for everything teachers and students do together" (2005, 1). Noddings (1984) also maintains that our relationships with learners form the foundation for successful pedagogical activity. As such, she emphasizes the importance of listening; engaging in dialogue about learners' needs, working habits, interests; and then designing plans for individual growth. In doing so, we grow in our competence as learners and teachers. Like Noddings, Raider-Roth posits that relationships shape our learning processes. Raider-Roth (2005) writes, "The fundamental relationships of school shape the ways that students learn to see themselves as effective participants in the learning process who have the capacity to develop their own ideas, articulate these ideas, and participate in collective thinking" (2005, 21–22). In parallel, in coaching relationships we want teachers to see themselves as effective participants in the learning process, developing and articulating their ideas, and participating in collective thinking. Teachers can then transfer understandings, instructional practices, and ways of being with learners to their teacher/student relationships and contexts.

A RELATIONSHIP EVOLVES

At 8:57 A.M. I gently tapped on the closed door and entered the second-grade classroom. As I walked in, Rose turned around and welcomed me with an enormous hug. We said in unison, "How are you? It's so good to see you!" Then she held out her left hand to show me an antique sapphire ring she was wearing on her pinky and asked, "Did you wear your mother's ring? I wore mine from my mother. I couldn't wait to show you." I had seen Rose a few weeks earlier, nine days after my mother died. During this visit, I had confided to her how much my mother's birthstone ring meant to me and how wearing it helped me get through the first difficult days after her death. But on this day in March as I entered the classroom I didn't remember that I had told her this, and I was honored by her compassion for me as we (re)connected over our mothers' rings and memories. What a welcoming beginning to my visit in her classroom.

We then briefly chatted about her mini-lesson. Rose had been discussing the importance of setting with her class and wanted to have her students attend to setting in the pieces they were writing. Today, she had prepared a mini-lesson on settings, based on a combination of two lessons she had read in *Craft Lessons*, by Ralph Fletcher and JoAnn Portalupi.

Over the previous few days, she and her students had talked about an experience they had shared with their book buddies called "Magic Carpet Reading." They noted that simply writing that the event had taken place in their elementary school gym would not convey the sight of the silvery, glittery streamers that had welcomed them as they entered the gymnasium, the towels strewn on the floor, the plastic baskets of books, the small carpets, the tall lamps with scarves draped over them, and the stuffed animals everywhere. Rose reminded her students that details would help readers envision the event they had so enjoyed. "Let's help our readers paint a picture in their minds of this party. Our PTA turned the gym into a magic carpet of reading. The details make a picture for the readers. That's our job as writers."

Rose then referred to a piece she had written earlier about a visit to the beach with her family as they dodged mounds of seaweed trying to find a clear spot to lay their towels. "If I just told you that I was at the beach, you wouldn't have a sense of the seaweed, the waves crashing. As writers, your readers want to hear more details. The details help your readers feel like they've jumped into your writing."

Rose asked her students to spend a few minutes conveying the setting of another class shared experience, a recent book swap held in Room 14. "What picture do you want to paint of this event? How would you describe the room?" As Rose passed out yellow Post-its for students to write on, they couldn't wait to make the book swap come alive.

The students wrote about the books at the book swap— books in boxes, books on chairs, books in bags, books stacked like pancakes, chapter books, Caldecott winners, fiction, nonfiction, picture books, series books stacked on top of one another. They wrote about the huge, rectangular tables labeled by grade level and the folding chairs they sat in as they read through and selected their books. They wrote about the balloons in the room ("I hadn't even remembered the balloons!" Rose said) and the blue "Books Are Magic" wristbands they were all given as they left the classroom. At the end of the mini-lesson, the students placed the Post-its in their notebooks as a reference for details and setting.

The evolution of our work together is constantly educative for me. This mini-lesson was in contrast to earlier times when Rose and I met together. Our early days were spent in conversations around more teacher-directed lessons. Rose, a veteran teacher of more than twenty years, said early on, "I'm a lifelong learner and I constantly self-evaluate, but it's different to do it with someone else. Allowing yourself to open up to someone and ask questions can be hard to do at first." Rose's openness and willingness to rethink and reconsider her teaching—always focusing on what was best for her learners—led us collaboratively to change instructional practices, often on the spot, and then to articulate those changes to each other and to her students. It was the trusting relationship we developed over time that led us to these exciting moments. Our professional relationship was not built in a day, a week, or a month. It was our sustained time together, our invested time together, that allowed us to build the trust and respect needed to ask questions, openly nudge and challenge each other, and then transfer our understandings to new instructional contexts.

HOW THE BOOK IS ORGANIZED

Chapters 2–5 offer a range of tools, both conceptual and practical, to use as you coach. The tools in Chapter 2 are designed to explore teachers' personal learning histories and to help coaches find teachers' zones of proximal development. In Chapter 3, the focus is on engaging in joint productive activities to extend and refine instructional practices and to analyze student work. The tools in Chapter 4 support examining language to build learning communities, to identify literate behaviors, and to consider the effect of our language choices. In Chapter 5, the tools help teachers build on their self-extending systems through collaborative conversations and inquiry. Chapter 6 broadens the coaching community to illustrate ways coaches develop partnerships with administrators and engage with families. Issues surrounding assessment and assessment practices are explored in Chapter 7. Chapter 8 attends to frequently asked coaching questions. Chapter 9 addresses sustaining change over time. Engaging with the tools helps teachers and coaches develop a relationship that creates and sustains lasting change. I hope this book becomes a welcoming and constructive tool in your professional life.

02 Sharing Our Literate Lives

After Lisa, an assistant superintendent, hired six new elementary teachers over the summer, we met to discuss how we would support their development as literacy teachers. Lisa and I decided that initially I would work with the new teachers over the course of several full-day sessions in the fall to develop a shared language with colleagues. During these days, I could learn about the areas the new teachers were most confident in teaching and also extend their repertoire of instructional practices. Whereas some of the teachers had several years of experience, others were newly graduated from college.

During our second day together, which focused on writing instruction, I asked the teachers to write about an experience in their schooling that changed them as learners in a positive or negative way (Routman 2005). To get everyone thinking about this focused piece of writing, I drew on one of my personal experiences. I described a difficult experience from eighth-grade French class when I was accused of giving answers to my classmates. After I talked about this episode and considered aloud how it had transformed me, we each shared school experiences before we began to write independently. The teachers described math experiences (both positive and negative), English teachers who supported them as writers and others who ripped up papers in front of classmates, the thrill of SRA kits in third grade, and Spanish teachers who called home to tell them they had passed a crucial exam for graduation. I had fully intended to write about my experience in French class until I listened to Melanie share her experience with SRA kits as a student. Listening to Melanie reminded me of another school moment for me, and I decided to write about my own experiences in sixth grade with SRA kits (not nearly as positive as hers!).

After we wrote, I invited people to share. "Who would like to share a line, a sentence, or your entire piece?" After some initial giggling and nervous shuffling of papers, Melanie shared the lead to her SRA experience. This led the other teachers to share their writing. All six said they appreciated the fact that they could choose how much or how little they would share with the group.

We then debriefed about the process, directions, and procedures of the literacy event. As we talked, we learned that we all liked the silence in the room for the first few moments of writing. We noted that the topic was pretty interesting and caused us to reflect on our school lives. Because we talked with one another about our topics beforehand, most of us readily engaged in the writing.

However, two people noticed how quickly some began writing and said this initially inhibited them. As we looked at our papers, we noticed who crossed out and whose papers looked "perfect"—no cross-outs, elegant handwriting. Everyone commented that they expected to have to share with the group, and that they thought about this as they wrote. Several changed their leads to make them more interesting. During our conversation, we learned the range of ways we had engaged with the task.

Then, we considered implications for classrooms. Based on the model, the teachers decided that share time could involve sharing a favorite word, a favorite sentence, and/or a sentence that needed some work. This was in contrast to their earlier ideas that students had to share their entire pieces of writing. Although all six teachers said they found the topic engaging, they wondered what would happen if students were given a topic they didn't embrace. Based on these concerns, we then explored what might happen if students didn't want to write about predetermined topics.

Engaging in this literacy event set us up as a community of learners and writers. We talked and problem-solved that day—writers to writers. As the day progressed, we revisited this literacy event again and again as we discussed instructional processes and procedures that worked for us— and didn't work for us—as learners, teachers, and writers.

THEORETICAL FRAMING: UNDERSTANDING HOW TEACHERS AND CHILDREN LEARN

Teachers and coaches bring their learning histories to their teaching. As Cole and Knowles (2000) remind us, "We teach who we are" (27). Our learning histories, often implicitly, guide and inform our views on teaching and learning. Cole and Knowles discuss the importance of examining our past experiences: "In remembering, re-creating, and writing about your prior experiences associated with learning, schools, classrooms, and teachers, you can make known the implicit theories, values, and beliefs that underpin your teaching and being a teacher" (28). Our learning histories are situated in cultural contexts where we interpret who we are in relation to others (Purcell-Gates 1995). Inquiring into our personal literacy histories allows us to gain insights and can "help us rethink our assumptions and beliefs" (Vinz 1996, 20) about teaching and learning. Through collaborative exchanges, we generate new understandings. The ways teachers think and their classroom behaviors are influenced by both their knowledge and their beliefs. For coaches to extend a teacher's professional knowledge base we must understand what the teacher knows and how the teacher learns.

Locating the learner's zone of proximal development (Vygotsky 1978) is central to responsive literacy coaching and to responsive teaching. Teachers, like their students, need support as they engage in new instructional practices. According to Gallimore and Tharp (1990), "A teacher cannot provide assistance in the zone of proximal development (ZPD) unless she knows where the learner is in the developmental process" (198). To locate where their students are, teachers make careful observations and then use the information to arrange for productive learning events. To discern where the teacher is, coaches make careful observations while teachers engage in learning events. These events "involve teachers both as learners and as teachers and allow them to struggle with the uncertainties that accompany each role" (Darling-Hammond and McLaughlin 1996, 203). Through the collaborative exchanges that follow, coaches and teachers learn from one another. This collaborative exchange offers ways of knowing learners.

The two tools in this chapter are designed to understand how teachers learn. The tools help literacy coaches locate teachers' zones of proximal development and offer windows into teachers' schooling and learning histories. The tools are:
- Engage in Literacy Events
- Sharing Our Literate Lives: Literacy Time Lines

TOOL 1: ENGAGE IN LITERACY EVENTS

Teachers As Learners

Having teachers engage in literacy events like the one described in the opening vignette is one coaching tool designed to explore and examine teaching and learning from the lens of a learner. During grade-level meetings or workshop sessions, I have asked teachers to respond to short stories, discuss nonfiction pieces, debate journal articles, sketch responses, engage in free writes, conduct book talks, or take portions of mandated state tests or assessments. Each event involves teachers in instructional experiences that can be adapted for their classrooms. Through engaging in these events, teachers become conscious of their own learning. Through the ensuing instructional conversations (Goldenberg 1992), I learn to follow the teachers' needs as learners. During these experiences, activities, and events, when teachers are positioned as learners, they also feel the range of emotions that accompany their learning.

I am deliberate in the instructional choices I make as I choose a literacy event for each session. As I prepare, I consider, for example, whether I will select a funny short story or something poignant for teachers to read and respond to. For each event, I also consider the level of risk-taking for the teachers. How comfortable are the teachers with one another? How comfortable are they with the writing process? Depending on the level of comfort, I might ask them to engage in a free write or a more focused write.

As teachers engage in the literacy events, they also note their preferred styles as writers. Some comment, "I never realized how hard it was to get started when I write. I looked around and saw others writing and got nervous." When I hear this, I remind teachers that on some days it is harder to start writing than on others. Watching others write can be daunting. It can propel you to write or shut you down. Teachers have said that experiencing the role of learner helps them better understand when their students experience writer's block.

Teachers talk about their engagement (or difficulty engaging). One kindergarten teacher commented, "I was nervous to write because I didn't know what *you* wanted." The first time a teacher shared this, I was taken aback. I hadn't intended for anyone to write what *I* wanted. It was a powerful learning moment for me. When this was followed by the comment, "I started off afraid to share because I didn't know if I had the right answer," I realized how deeply embedded the notion of a "right answer" is in our thinking and in our teaching. Quotes like these open doors for all of us to explore what it means to "be right." As a coach, I work hard to help teachers move beyond believing there are right and wrong responses and practices. Notions of right and wrong often lead to defensiveness and an unwillingness to reflect on instructional practices.

The benefit of working for a sustained amount of time with teachers is that as I come to know them well, I learn when to nudge and when to calm the waters so they can process and become comfortable and confident with new instructional practices. I share the deliberateness of each choice with teachers because I want them to be deliberate in their instructional practices with their students.

Discussion and Reflection—Process and Product

After completing the literacy experience, I ask the teachers to discuss both the process of engaging in the literacy event and the product created. As the teachers listen to one another, they hear their colleagues' reactions to the particular directions given and to the assignment itself. The conversation offers insights into the multiple ways in which all participants engaged in or "took up" the task. As one teacher noted, "I like it better when I get to choose how to respond. I don't like to draw or sketch, and I was nervous about this the whole time I was reading." Others in the group were surprised by her response. They found that the idea of sketching opened up possibilities they hadn't considered. Intentionally placing constraints opens the conversation to consider what happens in our classrooms when we reduce choices or provide no choices. I have always had groups of teachers with a range of reactions, so this discussion is always interesting. Some teachers like constraints or more structured events, whereas others find that it thwarts their level of engagement.

During these discussions, I am mindful to explore multiple options for teaching and learning. For example, "We approached [literacy event] this way. What are several other possibilities we could have tried?" "What else might you do? Why?" "What are the trade-offs? What are the benefits?" "What is left out if we decide to try…?" When teachers are asked to consider the complexities of teaching and instructional decision-making, they generate ways to move beyond one *right* answer, one *right* instructional practice in their classrooms. This encourages them to consider student involvement and achievement anew. In turn, as I listen to the teachers' responses, I learn how to respond to individuals during future coaching interactions. I use the insights gained from these learning events and the accompanying reflective conversations to become more responsive. Once teachers experience this responsiveness, I hope they will follow this model in their classrooms.

Classroom Implications

Next, we turn our attention to classrooms. During this time, the teachers articulate how literacy events might "look" in their classrooms. I ask, "What are the implications for your classroom? What would transfer to your classroom?" One teacher noted, "Every session you had us be learners. We had to write a response, sketch responses. One time we created a poem. We had to be learners. Then I started to think about what kids were thinking, how they might be feeling—to get inside their heads. Some [events] I liked better than others, and I was clear to you when I didn't like it. I like more structure. But listening to others, I realize some found the structure confining. That has made me more open. My kids are different, just like we [teachers] are. I need to remember this." Discussing the implications provides a powerful and important reflective space for teachers as they consider student engagement and achievement.

Envisioning Multiple Possibilities

"After the discussion today, what do you see as the possibilities?" "Where do you envision/How do you envision implementing…?" To acknowledge that taking on new practices can be difficult, I ask teachers to problem-solve. "What are the ways this might fall apart? What are the things that could happen that would cause [instructional practice] not to work? Let's look at this and problem-solve these together."

When teachers engage in literacy events, they assume dual roles: as learners and as teachers. Positioned as learners, they examine how they navigated the expectations and demands of the literacy event and articulate their needs as learners. Next, in the role of teachers, they consider the ways these literacy events are experienced and enacted by all participants. When we are in spaces as learners—where we must consider our zone of proximal development—we remember what it is like for students to be in their ZPDs.

Prompts

Here are several prompts I have used successfully during conversations around literacy events. After each one I articulate my rationale for the particular prompt. Consider extending this list with prompts that work for you as a coach.

- *What worked well for you as a learner?*
  When I ask this question, I learn how teachers approach the tasks. This provides a window into their thinking and offers me ways to work with teachers.

- *What didn't?*
  I learn so much. Do teachers prefer more structure or less structure? Were my directions vague or clear? What about my language? Was it invitational? Was the environment conducive or confining? What needs do teachers articulate?

- *What are the implications for your classroom?*
  This question is central to our work together. For
  all aspects of the literacy events, I want teachers to
  consider how our work together transfers to their
  classrooms.

- *How could the event(s) be modified for your classroom?*
  This question causes teachers to consider the range
  of ways the lesson or activity they experienced can
  be modified to fit their particular classroom needs. I
  always have a few more specific questions at the ready
  for teachers who might find answering this question
  difficult at first. For example, Would you provide more
  or less structure? Was the text level appropriate for
  your learners?

TOOL 2: SHARING OUR LITERATE LIVES: LITERACY TIME LINES

We bring our literate lives to our teaching and to our
coaching. Sharing literacy time lines encourages teachers
to explore their literate lives and experiences. Engaging
in conversations that center around teachers' experiences
as learners and their experiences in schools opens up
possibilities for coaches to consider the range of ways in
which teachers learn, their experiences as learners, and
the effect of both. As I listen to teachers, I discover ways to
support them based upon their experiences as learners.

The conversations around the literacy time lines are
compelling. Some teachers have no recollection of writing in
elementary school, whereas others reminisce about red pens,
book reports, summer vacation essays, and teachers who
celebrated (or didn't) pieces of writing. Others talk about
treasured pieces of writing or poetry kept by their mothers,
and contests entered. Some talk about learning to love to
write in school; others comment on experiences where they
shut down as writers. As readers, some talk about being

immersed in books. One recalled a mother who said, "Wait… until I finish this page, this chapter," which turned into "Wait until I've finished this book" and then noted that she now does the same thing with her boys. Some talk about reading groups named Cardinals and Snails and what it meant to be a cardinal or a snail, trying to get into the "top" reading group, what it meant to be in the middle group, hiding books within books to read uninterrupted during lessons, despising reading in elementary school, loving reading in elementary school, despising reading books in high school. Others quickly note memorable texts: *James and the Giant Peach, A Wrinkle in Time, Anne Frank, Number the Stars, Lord of the Flies,* a well-worn copy of *Danny and the Dinosaur,* Golden Books read on mothers' laps. Some teachers name themselves—"voracious reader," "vacation reader," "slow reader," "magazine reader."

Time-line conversations often turn to round-robin reading experiences and how some teachers loved to read aloud (though all agree it was never about comprehension, always about performance). One teacher talked about painful round-robin experiences, rehearsing reading aloud in front of a mirror to be ready for class to show the teacher that she truly *could* read, because reading aloud in front of other people made her incredibly nervous. Some talk about reading every word of every assignment, and others talk about skimming required texts yet devouring choice texts. Some teachers relax with books, whereas it would never cross others' minds to do so.

I also ask teachers to remember what it felt like to experience events on their time lines where they were honored as learners, or not. Some talk about their fascination with books, inspired by teachers who believed in them. Others recount listening in on conversations and being labeled as nonreaders when they knew they were readers— and setting out to prove the teacher wrong. Others recount when they were considered the good reader in the class—or when they weren't. One teacher recently noted, "I hated reading all through school, and I wanted to become a reading teacher to make sure other children didn't have my experiences as a reader. I want my students to love reading and want to read."

When teachers consider their histories as teachers of reading, they recall teaching from basal readers and developing lessons from the accompanying teacher's editions, conducting guided reading groups and learning how to level texts, teaching reading with nonfiction books, grading worksheets, developing centers for independent work, meeting authors and creating author studies, running literature circles, and learning to take and analyze running records. When exploring their histories as teachers of writing, they talk about initially floundering when they began to teach writing, moving from story starters to providing choices for students, writing on student work, never writing on student work, conferring, using status of the class (Atwell 1998) to develop mini-lessons, avoiding writing with their students, engaging in modeled writing.

After exploring the time lines, we turn our attention to implications for the classroom. Recently, implications included the power of choice. As teachers listened around the table, they noted that they were more willing to read when they were given choice, which led to the question, Am I providing enough opportunities for choice in my classroom? Several talked about abandoning texts, whereas others said that even as adults they still could not abandon texts. We talked about when and how children can abandon texts. Others recollected the power of the read-alouds they heard as children and wondered if *their* students would have read-aloud favorites from *their* classrooms. Because many of the teachers commented that once they were "in" a book, they were lost, we wondered together how, if, and when we were encouraging children to get "lost" in books. Often, teachers say considering their time lines is instructive, because they had not previously thought about how their experiences influenced their teaching. During these conversations, I also encourage teachers to share their literate lives with their students. In doing so, teachers and students begin to develop a reader-to-reader and writer-to-writer relationship.

Prompts

Here are several prompts I have used successfully during conversations around literacy time lines. After each one I articulate my rationale for the particular prompt. Consider extending this list with prompts that work for you as a coach.

- *What did you learn from developing your time line?*
  Asking this question opens the door to the teachers' thinking. Teachers share what they noticed and their experiences. I can then link the conversations to instructional practices in classrooms. In addition, teachers think about the multiple ways learners take up the instruction provided.

- *What are the implications for the classroom?*
  As teachers make connections between their lives as learners, they consider how these experiences transfer into their classrooms and affect their instructional decisions.

- *What surprised you about your time line? About the conversation?*
  Valuing surprise sets the table for learning from surprises. For example, a teacher recently noted during the conversation, "I had never realized how much I rely on what I did in school when I teach." Another teacher commented that she worked hard to avoid surprises in her classroom and liked the idea of learning from surprises rather than trying to avoid them.

- *How did you generate your time line?*
  I ask teachers to show each other the time lines they construct. It is always interesting to see the range of ways they generate their time lines. Some write

narratives, whereas others detail years, grade levels, and experiences on actual time lines, and others jot down memories.

CONCLUDING THOUGHTS

As teachers articulate and discuss their preferences and needs as learners, they consider what these preferences might mean for the learners in their classrooms. When this happens, the conversations shift. It is no longer about "right" or "wrong"; the focus shifts to learning, seeing, noticing, and collaborating. Wells (2000) reminds us, "It is by attempting to make sense with and for others that we make sense for ourselves" (58). When teachers write, they can appreciate the days when their children have writer's block, false starts, days when, as my high school Latin teacher, Dorothy Green, would say, "You've been inspired by the Muses." As writers, we engage with our students as writers. When teachers read, they know what it feels like to have thoughtful conversations about texts, consider multiple perspectives, enjoy and discuss authors' language, connect the texts to their worlds and life, and respond in multiple ways to texts. As readers, we engage with our students as readers. Helping teachers understand and problematize the range of ways they engage in learning events sets the table for thoughtful consideration and extending the repertoire of instructional practices in their classrooms.

03 Learning Together Through Joint Productive Activities

Michelle stopped me in the hallway one afternoon and asked if I would come to her first-grade classroom to help her analyze some of her students' writing pieces. As we sat down side by side with the writing samples between us, we talked about what we noticed—leads, attention to detail, interesting word choices, how the illustrations matched the writing, repetitive phrasing, endings. We talked about the strengths of each piece of writing and mini-lessons that had accompanied the pieces. We looked at several writing samples across students and then at writing across genres.

Then we turned our attention to the recently developed schoolwide writing benchmarks and chose a few pieces of writing to map onto them. After we individually highlighted the benchmark criteria on our own copies, we discussed our choices. We noted the similarities in our highlighted benchmarks. When we differed, we discussed our reasoning behind our choices. Sometimes we changed our minds. Other times we agreed to disagree.

The conversations and analysis of the writing samples led to a deeper understanding of writing and writing processes. Michelle and I inquired together to provide better instruction.

THEORETICAL FRAMING: ENGAGING IN JOINT PRODUCTIVE ACTIVITIES

When teachers and coaches inquire together, they form communities of practice (Lave and Wenger 1991). Participants share and develop knowledge and expertise when they engage in joint productive activities (Tharp and Gallimore 1988). Joint productive activities are shared events between coaches and teachers that result in the collaborative production of new learning. The collaborative nature of these activities extends the thinking and learning of everyone involved as coaches and teachers come to see teaching and learning with new eyes. In doing so, trust is gained and ongoing instructional relationships between and among participants are improved. As Tharp et al. (2000) remind us,

> *Joint activity is itself the single most sensitive and flexible point for school intervention in instruction and thus the most powerful means of affecting educational outcomes. To work together is to teach and learn together and to understand the world together. The effective design of instructional activity produces education through action, talk, work, and relationship. Social, intellectual, and community growth are enabled or crippled by patterns of joint productive activity (66).*

This chapter describes two coaching tools where coaches and teachers engage in joint productive activities (Tharp and Gallimore 1988). These tools can be used during one-on-one interactions, grade-level meetings, and larger group sessions. The tools are designed for working with and learning from teachers. The collaborative nature and design of the tools ensures that coaches and teachers inquire together. By using the tools, coaches and teachers together focus on literacy, literacy development, and exploring implications for classrooms. Engaging in the activities extends the thinking and learning of everyone involved as coaches and teachers come to see teaching and learning with new eyes. The two tools are:

- Team-Teach Lessons
- Examine Student Work

TOOL 3: TEAM-TEACH LESSONS

After reading her students' writing folders, Rose noticed that many included details that were not relevant to the writing pieces. In class, Rose frequently wrote about her daughter Lindsey's experiences, and her students loved hearing about Lindsey's many adventures. As she reflected on her writing about her college-age daughter, she noticed that she, too, included extraneous details in several places. Rose wanted to share one piece of writing that went off in several different directions.

Rose and I decided to team-teach a lesson on focusing pieces of writing. As she read her piece aloud, the students started to offer places she could eliminate or change the language and wording. At first, Rose tried to cross out and draw arrows—to no avail. Her piece was becoming increasingly difficult to read. I asked if we could use scissors to eliminate the extraneous parts and then tape the piece back together to check for coherence. Rose read her piece out loud. As she and her students located extraneous details, I cut. Then, with Rose rereading the piece aloud, I taped the piece back together. We added transition words where needed. We took the extraneous pieces and put them into a folder in case Rose wanted to use them later. We impressed to the students that these pieces could serve as writing topics on another day.

At the end of the mini-lesson, Rose asked the students to look in their writing folders and consider if there were pieces they thought needed to be more focused. "You might try cutting and taping," she said. "This might be a revision technique you want to use as a writer." As the students left for their seats, there was a chorus of, "Can we *really* cut our work?" "Oh, now I get why we only write on one side of our paper." "I'm going to try it. I hope I have extra details!"

Before students shared their work at the close of writer's workshop, we asked, "How many of you tried cutting and taping?" Several of the students who had tried this technique shared their revisions with the class. When we asked the students what worked for them as learners, they were eager to describe the ways they chose to cut and tape to revise. Rose and I conferred with the students and, as with all new techniques, we noted that several students overdid the cutting and pasting. We both knew that overusing the technique was all part of the students' learning (and our own).

Teaching lessons together creates opportunities to extend and refine instructional practices and to become more astute observers of children's literacy development. Teaching side by side also establishes a coach's credibility as a teacher. Team-teaching can take many forms—from team-teaching a whole-class lesson to working one on one, side by side with a teacher or a student.

Planning for the Lesson

When teachers and I sit together to plan the lesson(s), we are mindful of the following: the lesson content (the what), instructional practices to implement (the how), and the purpose and goal of the lesson (the why). First, I need to consider the expectations of the teachers as we teach lessons together. Am I here to teach a lesson? Analyze data together? Confer one on one with students? How much will I be "in" the lesson? Do I take a more active lead or should I be more of a support? How does/will our team teaching evolve? How can I create a collaborative space? Who talks and when during the lesson? Is it a back-and-forth exchange? What does turn-taking look like?

Through the ensuing dialogue, together we consider ways of approaching the team-teaching enterprise as well as potential pitfalls. This dialogue around the planning of the lesson(s) is central to our articulation of pedagogical possibilities and learning opportunities.

Teaching the Lesson

Teaching the lesson is the delicate orchestration of the earlier dialogue. These teaching moments are instructive for all—teachers, students, and coaches. It is within these lessons that we rethink our language choices, our pedagogy, and student engagement. Teaching with others opens up a wider offering of instructional possibilities. At the end of one team-taught lesson, a third-grade teacher commented, "I liked it when we bounced ideas off each other during the lesson. It's so much nicer to have two people in the room. I never would have thought about how Dylan was engaged. I saw him in a new way today. I'm so glad you found out that he likes writing about basketball. I didn't know that."

I couldn't agree more. Having two people teach together invites collaboration, attending carefully to what the students say and noticing what they need as writers.

Debriefing

When we debrief, I learn what the teacher valued from the teaching exchange. As part of the debriefing session, we also brainstorm multiple possibilities for future lessons. After jointly developing plans, we can determine what additional support would be beneficial.

After conducting a guided reading lesson in third grade, the teacher responded to the lesson, "I noticed that your book introductions are so much more detailed than mine. I always thought I'd give too much away. But you didn't give it away—you just helped them to read it on their own. They were so excited to get started." Comments like these are important for me as we work and develop lessons together. I believe book introductions are underused and underrated as instructional practices in schools. Book introductions offer an amazing range of instructional opportunities, as long as they are conversational. And yes, children are more excited about reading the books after engaging introductions. I often ask teachers how they determine what books they want to read and what gets them excited and interested in particular books. Then I ask them to develop their book introductions in similar ways.

I've also been asked, "How come it [instructional practice] seems so much easier when you're doing it? That's not fair." This question is hard for me to answer. I've often said, "I've had more practice," but it is much more than that. My teaching is intentional and deliberate—in following the lead of the learners. This can look seamless or "easy" to observers. However, my instructional decisions are deliberate as I work to stay within the learners' zones of proximal development. Given this, I ask teachers to look at the range of ways I followed the students' leads throughout the lesson and capitalized on what they said and did during and afterward.

I've had teachers ask, "Why don't you write a book with your exact language so I can say what you say when you're not in my room?" I remind them that following the lead of the learners (teachers and students) involves noticing how the learners—in this particular context, at this particular moment, with this particular text—"take up" the instructional moves, and my language follows their needs.

I want teachers to believe it is possible for them to be successful at implementing lessons, or the portions of the lessons I teach, so I am mindful of the importance of our debriefing time. It is always exciting to turn over the lessons and have the teachers take a more active role. When this happens, I am routinely asked, "What did you think? That's the first time I tried that." Analysis and reflection matter. Taking the time after lessons to consider what went well (and why!) and what could be changed are central to my responsiveness when I team-teach lessons.

Input from Students

We also seek input from the students. During and after team-taught lessons, the teacher and I ask the students, "What is working for you as a learner?" "What do you wish we had done differently?" Sometimes we stop for student responses in the middle of the lesson, whereas other times we request input after the lesson is complete. Our goal is to learn the range of ways students are taking up and learning from the instructional practices.

Lessons That Fall Apart

Lessons do—and will—fall apart. It is important to analyze the problems encountered, such as trying to cover too much content in one lesson, lack of engagement, and management difficulties. This reflective analysis encourages the joint development of future problem-solving strategies. Recently, I was asked, "What happened? That didn't go at all as we planned." Indeed. When the lesson fails (sometimes miserably), be clear about that and work to analyze the reasons with the teacher. This happened recently when I thought the students were more prepared for a lesson. I started in the middle (never a good idea), and even though the product ended up working, the principal said, "Cheryl, that was painful."

Changing Roles

As we spend more time in a range of classrooms, our roles change and the possibilities and our purposes for being invited to work with teachers increases. Like John-Steiner and Meehan (2000) note, "Increasingly we view collaboration as central to learning, to knowledge construction, and transformation" (43). Team-taught lessons can move beyond the more extensively planned lessons to serendipitous occasions as collegial relationships develop with teachers. For example, lessons can take on new and unexpected directions. Stopping in to say hello can lead to a quick mini-lesson. Visits to classrooms can lead to joining in during share sessions for writer's workshop or participating in read-alouds.

Prompts

Here are several prompts for teachers and coaches that I have used successfully to team-teach lessons. After each one I articulate my rationale for the particular prompt. Consider extending this list with prompts that work for you as a coach.

- *What are we hoping to accomplish during our lesson?*
  It's always easier to know what the expectations are before I begin. This way, if we aren't in alignment, I can repair—or move in a different direction. I can work to foster a common language as well.

- *Where are you in the curriculum in terms of [instructional practice]?*
  Where and how is this lesson situated in this classroom? What has happened before? What will follow? Gathering as much information about the classroom context, the expectations, and the teachers' and students' willingness to try new practices helps me be more productive.

- *What works best for you as a learner? As a teacher?*
  I don't ever want to put people on the spot. Some teachers like to join in, and others prefer to be silent. Some like to take the lead, some welcome surprises in lessons, and others don't. I like to know these things ahead of time.

- *Tell me about your students.*
  What do teachers say about their students? What do they notice? What matters to them? Teachers' responses

to this prompt provide a window into how they view teaching, learning, and children. Context matters. For instance, if the children are used to sitting in rows, it might be hard for them to sit in a circle and discuss their writing with one another. If this is an expected practice in the classroom, I can just move on with the lesson, versus teaching the students how to set up peer conversations.

- *What are some things I should know about your students as we prepare to…?*
  "They haven't had recess today." "We've changed the schedule; this isn't their normal writing time." These things matter. I meet these issues head-on and let the children know how much I appreciate their flexibility.

- *What worked for you? What didn't? What do you wish we had done differently?*
  These prompts open a conversation, a dialogue for future collaboration. Teachers and coaches together articulate their preferences and reflect on instructional practices. "I liked watching how the students responded to the mentor texts. They were so engaged." "I wish we had talked about the pace of the lesson. I always worry that mini-lessons become too long and then they don't have enough time to write." "I wish we had tried small groups first and then worked with the whole class. This way we could have refined it and then worked with everyone."

For students:

- *What's worked for you as a learner?*
  By asking this question, the teacher and I come to know the students as learners. It also helps the students articulate their needs and preferences. "I liked sharing with my partner." "I like having so many books in my browsing box." "I liked it after our group when we got to read the dialogue and act like the characters."

- *What would help you as a learner? What could we have done differently?*

These prompts provide opportunities for students to articulate their experiences as learners and offer a window into their learning. Their responses can direct the instructional opportunities we provide. "I needed more time." "I had a hard time finding information on the computer." "I wanted to pick my own book today." "It's hard working with my group." "Have more quiet time during writer's workshop." "More choices for when we're done with the book."

When I walk through the halls in schools, I am stopped by students who say, "Come up to my classroom and see my writing. I have to read it to you." Students also know I love books, so I hear, "I just read the newest Magic Treehouse book. Have you read it yet? Did you like it? I took the *Balto* book out of the library after reading it with you."

Team-teaching looks different based upon what individual teachers and coaches negotiate. It is important to be open to the range of ways teachers are ready to work together. The collaborative exchanges, with the multiple voices of the teachers, coaches, and students, extend the learning for everyone. As the relationships evolve, so, too, do the learning opportunities.

TOOL 4: EXAMINE STUDENT WORK

Walking past Erin's second-grade classroom I often noticed her huddled comfortably in a corner of the room working one on one with students. One day Erin stopped me in the hallway. She knew I helped other teachers analyze running records in my role as a literacy specialist and asked if I could help her learn how running records could inform her day-to-day reading instruction. I had a few moments available,

*so I immediately went into her classroom. We sat on
either side of her student, Jesse, and each administered
a running record. Afterward, we examined our
notations and then analyzed the errors. Together we
developed praise points and teaching points for Jesse.
When I left the room that day, we decided we would
continue our conversation.*

*Jesse was the first of many students we analyzed
together. With each new student, we extended our
understandings of running records and of Erin's
readers. We analyzed the texts read, prompts used,
and cueing systems used (or not). We noted where
Erin's readers were more fluent and when they
lost their stamina. We observed when students self-
corrected. Together, we continued to generate praise
points and teaching points. We problem-solved and
examined the range of strategies readers used in Erin's
classroom. Our conversations centered on seeking
ways to increase the students' literacy development.*
* -Susan Garnett*

A second joint productive activity grounds the
conversation in the work of the children. During one-on-one
meetings, grade-level meetings, or large-group workshops, I
ask teachers to bring a range of student work to discussions,
such as running records, writing samples, and responses
to literature. Examining student work gives a teacher an
opportunity to articulate what he or she knows about
literacy and literacy development. What does the teacher
discuss during the conversation? It could be the content of
the piece of writing, mechanics and conventions, or self-
corrections and repetitions. From these entry points, the
coach can determine the next phase and/or direction of
the conversation to support both student achievement and
instructional practices.

Focusing on the Strengths of the Learner

As teachers analyze student work samples, they are required to first look for positives. Insisting that teachers start with strengths sets up a discourse that is generative in nature. The initial emphasis with student work is to frame the example in what the child can do as a learner. In doing so, the discourse focuses on strengths rather than being driven by deficits. This can take practice. Early conversations discussing work samples include comments such as the following: "It's hard to focus on content. I get hung up if there aren't any capital letters or if there are words that are misspelled."

When teachers share that they initially see only the errors on a piece of writing when they are conferring with children, I recommend that they turn the papers over and let the children talk about the writing. Once teachers have received a piece of writing, they can focus on one or two productive teaching moments. In this way, the writers are not overwhelmed.

Over time, the conversations become more specific and detailed. This opportunity helps teachers become more astute in articulating the students' literacy development. It is always memorable to hear, "Look! This is the first time she ever self-corrected. How exciting is that?" Noticing the first self-correction is an exciting moment.

Considering the Instructional Practices

The conversations stay close to the details of the students' work as the teachers then theorize about different forms of evidence in different contexts. In this phase of the analysis, teachers consider the instructional practices that accompany the learning, such as the task itself, the directions given, the level of engagement, and the range of student responses. This examination includes the following: What was the child expected to do? What was the child's level of engagement?

Did the child write extensively in responses to the text, or respond with one- or two-word answers to questions? Consider the authenticity of the assignment. Were students engaged in thoughtful and productive work?

As we explore the differing demands of assignments, I hear comments such as this one: "I never realized how much the writing task itself matters. Look how much he writes here and look how little he wrote there." This is an opportunity to explore the fact that, yes, the writing task does matter. Is the writing the child is doing an assignment or something he or she has chosen to generate? How does the range of writing samples inform our teaching? How do the responses inform our understanding of the child as a learner?

As the teachers analyze their running records for individual children and across their classes, they come to notice which cueing systems children use most extensively. "My prompts are becoming more specific on my running records. I used to say the same thing every time. Now I'm noticing that I use more prompts." Are we providing opportunities for students to read and write for real purposes? Authentic and meaningful opportunities matter for student engagement and for sustaining motivation.

Prompts

Here are several prompts to examine work samples. After each one I articulate my rationale for the particular prompt. Consider extending this list with prompts that work for you as a coach.

- *What can this child/reader/writer do?*
  It is often easier to see what children struggle with, but our job as coaches is to help teachers articulate what our students can do, and in what instructional contexts. This prompt encourages the teacher to consider both the learner and the instructional opportunities provided in the classroom.

- *What are the strengths of the reader? What strategies is the child using? Point to a place where you noticed...*
  This prompt insists that the teacher articulate the many strategies the child uses as a reader. Does the child self-correct? Does the child pause and reread when coming to a difficult word? Does the child read fluently? As the teacher articulates these strategies, she becomes more alert to them and starts to name them for the student. It also changes what the teacher focuses on in terms of literate competencies. This language helps the teacher notice what the children are doing and are not (yet) doing and how he or she is instructing or not (yet) instructing.

- *What are the strengths of the writer? The piece of writing? Point to a place where you notice...*
  Again, this prompt speaks to the necessity of pointing to specifics in the writing samples for examples that illustrate the points raised in the discussion. "Look at the range of leads in these three writing pieces." "Notice how the writer uses interesting endings." "This is the first time Susan used punctuation in her writing—and she used three punctuation marks in the same sentence!"

Prompts That Focus on Instructional Practices

- *Talk about the differing demands of the writing samples you brought.*

- *What were the differing demands of the writing tasks used?*

- *What are the demands of the text you just read?*
  It is important to bring teachers' attention to the expectations and demands for each genre for reading and writing. Some students find fiction more engaging, whereas others gravitate toward nonfiction texts. Some

students find personal narrative easier, and others prefer to write nonfiction.

The above prompts ask teachers to do several things at once—articulate the strengths of the learners and consider the teaching opportunities they provide in their classrooms. The specificity of the responses helps them move beyond impressionistic views of their learners.

Analyzing student work grounds the conversation in the strengths of the learners. During these conversations, coaches and teachers also examine how different instructional tasks are taken up by the students. By engaging in this joint productive activity, teachers' relationships with their students change. The more you notice, the more you see. Children are seen through the lens of strengths, versus more deficit-driven theorizing.

The tools described in this chapter advocate learning as a collaborative enterprise through joint productive activities. Together, teachers critically examine teaching and learning while building relationships with their colleagues and their students. "If we, as educators, are to change the vision of the next generation of teachers concerning schools, then we must exemplify that vision in joint productive activity" (Tharp and Gallimore 1988, 273). In the next chapter, we turn our attention to language.

04 Examining Language

Diana invited me into her first-grade classroom for the first day of her Unit on Study on Revision (Calkins 2003). As her students joined her on the rug, Diana welcomed them and told them they were about to try something new as writers. "You're going to make your very best writing even better. Today, we're going to revise something you've written. In your writing folders you will find a piece of your writing that has been photocopied. When you revise, you can write right on your paper." To revise, each student had a "new tool" in the writing folder—a blue pen. "This is a writing tool," Diana said. "It will stay right in your folder for revising."

Diana then said she would revise a story she had written earlier in the year. "Remember the time I told you that it was rainy and I was running late and I fell in a puddle? My dad laughed, even though I was late. I had to change my clothes and get dry." As Diana recounted this piece of writing with her class, they giggled, with numerous students noting, "Hey,

I remember that." Her earlier piece of writing was written on three sheets of chart paper, with accompanying illustrations. "The first thing I need to do is reread. Then, I need to make a plan in my head. I want to start to think, How will I make it better? What will make it more interesting for my reader? I want my reader to think, I can't wait to see what will happen next."

Diana then asked her students to turn to the person next to them and talk about what she might add to her piece of writing. "I know that I shared more with you than I wrote. What might I add?" Immediately, one student turned to his partner and said, "She needs to add details to make it more interesting." Another child commented, "She needs to add what she was thinking. She should also add about her dad." Another wondered aloud, "Did you hurt yourself when you fell?"

After a few moments, Diana brought the group together and listened to her students' suggestions. She decided to include the fact that her dad giggled when he saw her and that she was surprised she had fallen over such a tiny rock. She also included her class's favorite craft feature, the speech bubble, with her dad saying, "Ha ha!"

Together, they made a chart to post in the classroom:

Writers Revise

1. Reread.

2. Make a plan.

3. Add words.

4. Add to our pictures.

Then, with writing folders, photocopied pieces of writing, and new blue pens in their hands, the students were off to their tables. Every child was excited to revise. Every child in the classroom loved having a pen—a novelty! Each child eagerly met Diana's challenge: "As writers, make your great writing even better."

When I sat down next to Khaleeq, he decided to focus on his illustration, noting the clock he had drawn with the time, 7:45. When I asked what made 7:45 so important, he said, "That's fifteen minutes before I have to go to bed. I should add that." And he did—with his new blue pen. Diana was at a nearby table reading a piece with another student. As she conferred, she said, "You know what I love? I could tell how much it mattered that you lost a tooth. You used an exclamation mark!"

When I sat with Tanya, who was writing about her aunt's varied and extensive collection of pets, I wondered, "Who thinks your aunt has too many pets?"

"Everyone in my family, but not my aunt!" She quickly went to the stack of writing paper to get another sheet to add this information.

These first graders revised by adding details to their writing and adding to or including illustrations. They also edited as they attended to punctuation and looked at the word wall for conventional spellings. As writer's workshop neared the end, Diana selected several students to share with the class. When they shared, she reminded them, "Read your piece of writing. Then, talk a little bit about what you did to make your piece even better."

After Thomas read his piece about getting hurt on the playground, Diana said, "Thomas, tell your friends what you did. Then I'll add what I noticed."

Thomas was excited as he said, "I wrote more stuff than I did last time."

Diana then added, "I noticed that Thomas added details and included his feelings. He added what the nurse did for him that made him feel better."

Sasha changed her punctuation, asking Diana, "Can I cross out my period to make my sentences longer?" Sasha also added dialogue: "That's a lot of money for a little tooth."

The next student displayed the pictures she added as Diana commented, "Today your friend added some pictures. She didn't have pictures before." Writer's workshop ended with Diana saying, "Tomorrow, you'll have a chance to revise again. I can't wait to see what you write."

Diana named her students as writers. *Every* student in her class was a writer. *Every* student viewed his or her teacher as a writer. Through Diana's careful and deliberate use of language and her genuine interest in her students and their developing literate competencies, these first graders embraced writing and their identities as writers.

THEORETICAL FRAMING

We use language to make sense of our selves and our world. Delpit (2002) asserts, "Since language is one of the most intimate expressions of identity, indeed, 'the skin that we speak,' then to reject a person's language can only feel as if we are rejecting him" (47). Given that we internalize the types of conversations with which we become involved, as teachers and coaches we should seriously consider "the nature of these school interactions and their implications" (Johnston 2004, 65). As such, examining our language choices is a powerful tool for responsive literacy coaching and responsive teaching. McNaughton (2002) concurs: "The ways in which a teacher teaches carry messages about roles and relationships within the classroom, about what counts as learning, and about what are appropriate uses of language" (69). As coaches and as teachers, our language choices matter.

Language is also a means by which we generate understandings, explore together, inquire together, and learn together. Lyons, Pinnell, and DeFord (1993) remind us, "Conversation must assume a prominent role in teachers' learning. Transactions take place and higher cognitive processes are initiated and instantiated through dialogue" (164). By engaging in dialogic conversations, we can consider anew our instructional practices and student learning. Exploratory talk offers a way for teachers and coaches to deliberately consider and analyze their language choices. Mercer (2000) notes the importance of engaging in exploratory talk, acknowledging that participants "must not be primarily concerned with protecting their individual or joint identities and interests, but instead with discovering new and better ways of jointly making sense" (102–103). Engaging in explicitly noticing and naming (Johnston 2004) literate work, literate behaviors, and literate processes serves multiple purposes—from developing shared understandings, to articulating what literate processes we have control over, to determining what is worthy of noticing, to examining the effect and consequences of our language choices. The four tools in this chapter intentionally turn our attention to language. The tools are:

- Communicating with Others
- Selecting and Sharing Texts
- Naming Our Literate Work, Processes, and Strategies
- Sharing and Naming Celebrations

TOOL 5: COMMUNICATING WITH OTHERS

Our interactions matter—from the quick hello in the hallway, to the sustained conversation as a teacher rethinks writing instruction, to the memo we hastily send out to our colleagues. As coaches we want to consider the effect and consequences that our language choices have on others. Does our language invite teachers to participate? What language makes teachers reluctant to participate? When we send out bulletins, memos, and e-mails, we want to be conscious of our language and mindful of our tone. Does the tone embrace the intent or (inadvertently) work against the intent? As Deborah Tannen (2006) cautions, we want to recognize the message we send as coaches, as well as the "metamessages." Are we responsive in our communication? Do we quickly and thoughtfully respond to others, if only to say that we will get back with a more detailed response at a later date? Do we acknowledge the importance of each of our coaching interactions? These questions put language choices front and center in our coaching.

Understanding the histories of the teachers in the buildings where we work allows for better communication. Understanding the histories of previous change agents in the district and building and how they were received also provides insights into how to communicate with others. As coaches we need to listen carefully to understand the dynamics and hidden agendas that can potentially sabotage our work.

Are we running training sessions? Are we inviting or forcing learning? Are we organizing book clubs? Are we holding conversations? Are we implementing mandates? Are we constructing rubrics? Are we monitoring assessments? Are we engaging in collaborative inquiry? Are we creating learning spaces that are dialogic in nature? Are we mindful of what and how we are "naming" our learning spaces with teachers? All of these choices are value laden. All speak to our theoretical constructs for language, literacy, and learning.

Training is a term used freely in professional development and remains relatively uncontested. But the terms *training* and *teaching* are more than word choices. Hoffman and Pearson (2000) addressed this issue and examined the theoretical underpinnings of teaching and training. *Training* implies a program or a package you impart. The use of the word *training* does not honor or acknowledge choices that teachers make professionally. I want training in CPR and the Heimlich maneuver. But when it comes to working with teachers and children, I want to use my professional judgment to make teaching decisions as I consider the learner, the context, and the task.

TOOL 6: SELECTING AND SHARING TEXTS

As we consider text choices that we use as coaches, whether professional readings for teachers or texts that we recommend for students, we want to ask, What do the texts we choose say? What messages do we send with our text selections—read-alouds, shared reading, guided reading, browsing boxes for independent reading, and mentor texts for writing? What texts do we privilege? Are we choosing books in which students see themselves represented? Are we finding books that will encourage a lifelong love of reading and language? Are we introducing students to a range of genres? Why and how do our text selections matter?

Because they do matter. Recently, fourth and fifth graders in a city school district were asked where they spend most of their time reading. All but the most successful readers, in every case, answered, "in school." Given this, we need to carefully and purposefully consider and examine the texts we offer.

When I am working with teachers, I include a read-aloud in each session. A current favorite is the book *ish* by Peter Reynolds (2004). This book is a wonderful text to encourage teachers who are starting to make changes to the way they teach writing and rethinking their writing instructional practices. This picture book celebrates pushing past conventional boundaries and not being afraid to try new things. In *ish*, Ramon believed he was an artist until his brother laughed at his drawings because they did not look "right." Through his sister's encouragement Ramon returns to his art and becomes a writer as well.

> *Ramon felt light and energized. Thinking ish-ly allowed his ideas to flow freely…His ish art inspired ish writing. He wasn't sure if he was writing poems, but he knew they were poem-ish (Reynolds 2004).*

Once teachers hear this book, they include it in their picture book and mentor text collection. Recently, during status of the class (Atwell 1998) in Caryn's second-grade classroom, a student said, "I'm middlish to the end of my piece of writing." Afterward, Caryn shared that she had received the book as a gift. To start writer's workshop in September, she had read the book to her class, and she was delighted when the students appropriated the language from the text.

Alice the Fairy by David Shannon is a fabulous book for encouraging children (and their teachers!) to take risks as writers. Shannon is playful—as an author and as an illustrator. This book encourages children to experiment with placement of text on the page, dialogue, and creating their own language. That Shannon has fun with language is abundantly clear.

When I read aloud to teachers, and students, I name what I find interesting in the text. While reading *Odd Velvet*, I stop, pause, take a breath, and say, "And here is my favorite line in the book: 'Velvet brought in a milkweed pod for show and tell. Luckily, three of the other girls brought in a talking doll, a wetting doll, and a crying doll, and saved the day.'" I love Mary Whitcomb's humor, her use of language, and the contrast she presents between Velvet and the other girls in her class. As the book continues, the children come to understand that Velvet's ways might not be so odd after all.

As a mentor text for writing, I often use *In My Momma's Kitchen* by Jerdine Nolen. The lead, "Seems like everything good that happens in my house happens in my momma's kitchen," is a favorite. The beauty of the language and the power of Nolen's words as she expresses family love are captivating. When working with fifth-grade teachers recently, I used *Al Capone Does My Shirts* by Gennifer Choldenko as a mentor text. This book has the most satisfying ending of any book I've ever read—an ending that is to be savored. When the book arrived at the school book fair, it immediately sold out.

I am also mindful to select a range of genres for my read-alouds and to share the thinking behind my selections. In this way, I model purposeful book choices and a range of possibilities for read-alouds in classrooms.

TOOL 7: NAMING OUR LITERATE WORK/PROCESSES/ STRATEGIES

As I walked into Michelle's first-grade classroom on a cold January morning, she called her students together to the blue oval rug in front of the easel. The easel was the centerpiece of her spacious room—a gathering place for mini-lessons and sharing. On this day, Michele asked her students to think about the text features they noticed in *Miss Malarkey Doesn't Live in Room 10*, by Judy Finchler. She began her mini-lesson with the question, "Think for a moment. What does Judy Finchler do in this text that we do as writers?"

At first, the room was silent. After waiting a few moments, Michele said, "I'll help you get started. Her writing makes sense." That was all her students needed to hear.

"Oh, oh," the children chimed.

"She uses interesting language."

"Yes, she does. What else does she do that we do as writers?" The hands went up, and the children continued to call out.

"She uses details."

"Her writing matched the pictures."

One student noted, "Some words were darker." This led to finding the place in the text where the font was, indeed, darker, which led to, "You can tell when she *really* meant it."

"She has dialogue. Two people were talking," Mark said.

Michelle then commented, "Just like you, Mark. You used dialogue in your writing last night."

Another student offered, "She has the gift of neat handwriting," which led to a conversation about computers and font styles. As the discussion came to a conclusion, another student added, "It was an interesting ending because it was a happy ending."

Michelle's first-grade students had appropriated the language of writers. They noticed and named the craft features in Finchler's text.

Naming It

Naming sets the table for a shared literacy, for shared understandings. Although Michelle's example relates the naming of craft features, the naming (or lack thereof) of conventions can also influence literacy learning. In one district, during a joint kindergarten/first-grade-level workshop, we found that teachers in kindergarten were saying, "Be sure to use a capital letter." In first grade, the teachers told the students, "Use an uppercase letter at the beginning of each sentence" and were surprised when the students didn't know (initially) what they were expecting. One of the teachers was surprised when a student asked her, "You mean a capital letter?" As the conversation continued, some teachers remarked that they reminded their students to put periods at the end of sentences, whereas others told their students to put the "stop mark."

The same issue was raised in several discussions from a primary building to an intermediate building around topic sentences and paragraphs. Are we teaching leads or are we teaching students to write topic sentences? How are these different? How are they similar? When do we name a group of sentences a paragraph? In kindergarten? Later? When and how does this matter? Engaging in ongoing dialogue about these language issues and questions avoids the "Don't they teach any mechanics or conventions at *that* grade level?" conversation stopper.

The fact that students find some terms unfamiliar does not mean they do not know what they are doing—it may simply mean the students are unfamiliar with the terms. What is our goal and/or purpose for using particular literacy terms? Do we explicitly discuss these terms with our students—and each other? Sustained dialogue about language choices ensures that children will have a smoother transition— from grade level to grade level and building to building. Explicitness matters. Naming matters.

We not only invite teachers to name craft features and their literate processes and strategies, but also want them to share and name celebrations that occur within their classrooms and that transfer to other settings.

TOOL 8: SHARING AND NAMING CELEBRATIONS

The conference room was abuzz with the sharing of stories as several new teachers in the district described instructional practices they had tried out after their first session on guided reading the week before. As the clock turned to 8:40 A.M., I began our second daylong workshop by saying, "Let's start with celebrations." This opening was clearly a surprise for the teachers. I noted the silence, the nervous shuffling of papers, the downcast eyes.

The silence was in direct contrast to earlier moments when the teachers were talking excitedly about their book introductions, the new texts they were using in their classrooms, and the children's responses to the Post-its they were using. Since teachers had included me in their earlier conversations, I could draw from those examples to start with celebrations. I let the teachers know that each time we worked together, we would begin our conversations with celebrations—of their teaching and of their students' literacy development. "Think about the conversations we were just having. Those were such celebrations. Marti, you said you were surprised at how much your students enjoyed the leveled readers."

Krystina began the discussion. "Now I know what guided reading is. It was easy to follow the framework."

Annette followed, noting that she had encouraged her students to read silently for the first time. "I slipped behind them as they were reading silently. I listened to them read aloud a bit and then moved to another person in the group. When we came together [after reading silently], I had them choose their favorite parts to read aloud. I also introduced the vocabulary words inside the text for the first time."

Brianne noted that she had tried to incorporate the organizational framework for her guided reading block that we had discussed the week before, which included students engaging in a guided reading lesson, responding to the text, reading from the browsing box, and listening to stories in the listening center. She commented, "I feel like the structure can be done." Eliza noted that she had focused on improving her book introductions, and Marti said that "naming the strategies" had worked for her students.

Starting with celebrations reframes the way we think about teaching and learning. Through celebrations, teachers name the range of ways they are extending and refining their instructional practices and the range of ways their students are growing and developing. It also identifies the teachers' zones of proximal development. As a coach, it shows me where each teacher's attention is, what she is noticing, and where and how she is ready to grow.

As teachers recognize that our interactions always begin with a celebration, they come to look for celebrations in their classrooms and begin to name them. Celebrations are joyful and take on many forms—from describing instructional practices that have gone well, to naming ways students are developing literate competencies, to discussing research that confirms practices, to offering personal celebrations.

Consider the following examples from the University at Albany Literacy Lab where teachers share how their one-on-one tutorial work in the lab transferred to new situations in their classrooms (Bransford and Schwartz 1999). Teachers commented that through the celebrations, they began to notice and articulate the positive things happening in their classrooms and tutoring. The predictability and structure of the tool also nudged the teachers to see how a one-on-one tutorial could transfer to a setting with twenty to thirty children.

> *Jane: I've made a chart for myself of all the prompt questions to use while they're reading. Now I'm using a range [of prompts] instead of just one or two.*
>
> *Laura: One of my students was stuck on a word and I gave her wait time, and so did the other students. Then she got it [the word].*
>
> *Shireen: I'm becoming sensitive to where the children might be having problems with the text.*
>
> *Melissa: In my guided reading groups the conversation is so much more natural. I'm seeing a change in myself.*
>
> *Leann: I rearranged the reading books by levels and helped my students preview vocabulary words before we began.*
>
> *Brooke: I did a book introduction for the first time the way we talked about. What a difference!*
>
> *Suzanne: I loved the strategies bookmark. I've put them in their zipper bags to take home each night.*
>
> *Nancy: We talked about critical literacy in my classroom, getting the kids to think of different opinions, thoughts, and views. Even in small books [leveled readers] we can engage in critical literacy. Our children's lives may not match up with the books we have. That's one place to start.*
>
> *Meagan: The other kindergarten teachers are starting to come to me and asking me about running records. I feel good about that.*

Celebrations occur on multiple levels—the naming and articulation of instructional practices and student learning as well as the relational aspect of our work together. This can be seen when many of our meetings and sessions begin with engagement announcements, birth announcements, and passing pictures of children around the table. Celebrations frame the day and the interaction and become a way of being together. After the first time together, teachers come to our interactions prepared to share. Debbie began one session, "I have to go first before I forget. Now my triplets and I start our dinner together each night with celebrations."

When working one-on-one with a teacher, I help the teacher notice and name celebrations. If we team-teach a lesson, I initially name productive moments. For example, I model by saying, "Notice how engaged your students were during their writing time." "Look at the range of responses to..." "I noticed how independent your kindergartners were during center time." "Every one of your students made a text-to-text connection during your book introduction." After this modeling, I turn over the naming to the teacher.

Starting with celebrations can be difficult if teachers think they are "bragging" or are not used to looking at children's (and their own) strengths. Changing the discourse can be discomforting. As Florio-Ruane and Raphael (2001) remind us, asking teachers to engage in conversation-based learning can be challenging because most have not experienced it as part of their learning histories. Cook-Sather (2001) points out that there may be tensions between what is familiar and what is new. I've said on more than one occasion, "Is that a celebration?" and worked to move the conversation to a more productive or positive path. If teachers are reluctant to share with a group, I use the same strategy I use with reluctant writers during writer's workshop. I share something that happened in a classroom and then turn the floor over to one of the teachers, with others asking questions about the logistics and practicalities involved in implementing the lesson. In this way, teachers articulate how they implemented the practices. What is especially exciting is when teachers who do not initially see themselves as leaders start to name the productive learning spaces in their classrooms, and other teachers ask to know more.

Prompts

These are prompts I've used to invite teachers to celebrate their teaching and student learning:

- *As we begin our conversation today, let's start with celebrations.*

- *Celebrations first.*

  By using the prompt "Let's start with celebrations" I ask teachers to look for their teaching strengths and the strengths of their students. Whether I work one on one with a teacher, with a grade level, or with a larger group, this prompt insists that we all consider what is working and that we focus on strengths—first. This prompt also leads me to understand the teachers' zones of proximal development. From the noticings and celebrations, I can provide nudges to move the teacher forward.

  This is not to say that I don't recognize that engaging in new instructional practices can be hard—it is. However, regardless of how difficult or stressful new teaching practices are, we first examine positive teaching and learning moments to move the learners (teachers and students) forward.

Considering language is of paramount importance for coaches. Language humanizes us—or dehumanizes us. We are positioned through language and position others with our language choices (Johnston 2004). As we communicate with others, we examine the texts we choose, our language choices, and the consequences of these choices for teachers and students. Engaging in conversations with colleagues is important for continuing professional development (Clark 2001). In naming literate processes and strategies we "develop teachers' conceptual understandings about the reading and writing processes" (Lyons 2002, 93). By sharing and naming celebratory spaces in our teaching and student learning, teachers extend and refine their instructional practices.

05 Developing Self-Extending Systems

Lora's second-grade classroom is a celebration of inquiry. Her students love science and so does she. One bulletin board contains a photo from a local newspaper of Lora helping endangered salamanders cross the road in the middle of the night. On this March afternoon, Lora began her mini-lesson by saying, "Remember, you are promising to teach your readers about your subject in your All About Book." She used the Gail Gibbons text *The Pumpkin Book* to illustrate the range of ways authors can organize texts. After reading the text to the class, Lora asked, "What kind of ideas does this book give you for your All About Books? As writers, we can look at published authors to help us get ideas. If the ideas in this book don't help you, remember you can go to the bin with our other All About Books to get some ideas."

After discussing the diagram of the pumpkin seed in the text, Lora turned on the overhead to a diagram of an ant from *Weekly Reader* magazine. "Although none of you has chosen insects, we can still see how the details help us understand the parts of the ant. Remember, these are parts of a diagram, and the parts are labeled. When you include a diagram, you are promising to teach about the part of the subject you are drawing." Lora asked her students to close their eyes and imagine their subjects (Mercury, Pluto, Saturn, the sun, cheetahs, lions, sharks, and giraffes) and to think about parts they would include in a diagram. "Think about what is really important to teach your reader," she said.

Next, Lora asked the children to turn to a partner and talk about the parts they would include for a diagram. Initially there was some hesitation, but within a few moments, the room was filled with, "Ah...now I get it. Oh, I'm going to include... Me, too. No, that won't work for my book." As the students got ready to leave the rug to go write, Lora reminded them, "When you are writing, writers pause and think about the tools they need for writing. Think, What kind of paper do I want to use to organize my thoughts? What kind of paper do I need to organize my writing for my readers? You can try out this paper and see if it works for you. Remember, we are teaching our readers about our subjects."

After the mini-lesson, the students conferred with Lora and with one another as they drew their diagrams. Some of them needed more information and logged on to Lora's school Web site to conduct their research via www. worldbookonline.com, www.enchantedlearning.com, and www.windows.ucar.edu. Lora reminded them, "If this isn't the type of paper you want to use, you can create or invent your own paper. Writers pause when they finish a paper and decide what they need next."

The independence Lora fosters and the self-extending systems she nurtures encourage her students to think beyond the boundaries. She invites them to create their own paper and to make decisions about their learning. Lora provides models but does not confine her students to these models.

Her language includes, "What do you think would work for you? What do you think is missing? What would help you?"

THEORETICAL FRAMING: SELF-EXTENDING SYSTEMS

Developing self-extending systems to generate and sustain learning is the goal of responsive literacy coaching and teaching. Self-extending systems are developed and continuously redeveloped through collaborative inquiry and conversation. Just as teachers support students to develop self-extending systems (Clay 1991; 2001), literacy coaches can support teachers to "acquire reasoning skills that enable them to construct a self-generating system for making powerful teaching decisions" (Lyons, Pinnell, and DeFord 1993, 170). Self-extending systems are generative: coaches and teachers collaboratively engage in problem-posing and problem-solving and seek ways to promote sustained learning for teachers and students. For coaches and teachers, "building a self-extending system entails setting up the conditions where teachers notice, theorize, productively (self-) critique, and build a sustaining learning community" (Dozier, Johnston, and Rogers 2006, 33). These learning communities provide intellectual spaces for coaches and teachers to engage in collaborative inquiry, to construct understandings, to enact pedagogy, to examine language choices, and to articulate pedagogical decision-making. Coaches and teachers will notice shifts over time as teachers transfer their understandings flexibly and competently into new contexts.

The tools in this chapter are aimed at fostering learning communities among teachers. The tools are:

- Study Groups
- Transcribing Lessons and Conferring with Teachers
- Visiting Colleagues' Classrooms
- Extending the Learning Community: Sharing Knowledge

TOOL 9: STUDY GROUPS

Study groups can take many shapes, depending on teachers' needs and interests. Some teachers and coaches prefer to start study groups with children's literature, whereas others begin with professional readings. There are numerous possibilities for constructing and organizing study groups—inquiry around texts, inquiry around instructional practices, and inquiry around teaching and learning. Study groups have met at restaurants, in homes, in classrooms, and in conference rooms. Study groups can meet for breakfast, for dinner, or after school. When we meet in restaurants, we are sure to ask for a space where we can talk, because we usually get quite noisy! I believe good things happen around food, so I am sure to organize food whenever we meet.

Study groups can be set up as a sequence for the entire year where teachers can "dip in and dip out," depending on what is happening in their lives. Other study groups can build on learning from the previous year. Decisions are often based upon the needs (and finances) of the teachers and the district.

By participating in study groups, teachers build on their self-extending systems by engaging in collaborative learning and intellectual inquiry with others. Study groups encourage, support, and promote teachers' professionalism and instructional decision-making. The instructional conversations in study groups inevitably lead teachers to new places, new understandings, new possibilities, and new instructional practices; that is the beauty of the learning that is involved in this professional dynamic. Next, we explore several types of study groups, beginning with a vignette by Susan Garnett.

To examine and discuss new texts available in our building, I invited teachers to take an after-school "field trip" to the book room. To organize for the teachers' visit, I showcased newly purchased books by displaying them on large tables and categorizing them by genres. I invited teachers to read, talk, and explore books of their choice. After reading the books, the teachers engaged in a conversation identifying the range of genres and discussing possible ways they could use the books for writer's workshop, guided reading, or read-alouds. As I listened to the teachers, I heard, "Hey, I might use this for my memoir study. I didn't realize this book was a memoir before today. It was nice to see biographies and memoir side by side." "I never thought about using this book for point of view." "Now I've got several books for good leads." "Look at the great language in this text."

The librarian joined our conversation and, after looking at the new texts and listening to the teachers, decided to include more accessible and interesting biographies in her library collection. Some of the teachers who in the past had used only one text for the whole class found books on similar topics at a range of levels. Teachers who might not have gone to the book room individually told me that their conversations about the texts opened doors for new ways to use them in classrooms. Through this "field trip" teachers added new texts to their classrooms and explored instructional possibilities for those texts— all the while reinvigorating interest in and finding multiple uses for our book room.

–Susan Garnett

Bookstore Study Group

In one building, teachers representing several grade levels traveled together to bookstores to buy books. Before going to the bookstores, they examined their book room and looked for gaps in terms of genre selection and texts available for guided reading levels. With their specific needs in mind, they purchased books together. To decide which ones to select, the teachers talked about the possibilities they saw in each book, ways they could use the text, and how the book would extend their current collection in the building (or their classrooms). They then presented the new books during a faculty meeting. Just as in classrooms when teachers read books aloud to their students, the books from this book talk became the coveted selections from their book room.

Instructional Practices Study Group

In another study group, teachers brought successful instructional practices to share with others. Teachers have shared word study activities, center work or independent work for students during guided reading, browsing boxes, poetry journals, mentor texts for writer's workshop, PowerPoint presentations on metamorphosis, Web site explorations, and Web site addresses where students can publish their written work. Teachers can question one another, connect to their classroom instruction, reflect on their teaching, and extend current practices. This is another opportunity for teachers to articulate their instructional decision-making and consider the ways students engage in the learning opportunities offered.

Children's Literature Study Group

I have organized children's literature study groups when teachers wanted to gather to read children's books, talk about them, and consider ways to include them in their classrooms. In one group, we all read the same text and then generated instructional possibilities to engage the children as they read the book. Several teachers wanted to focus on vocabulary instruction, so we selected vocabulary words central to the text. Others wanted to focus on issues around themes in the text. For another study group, we all read different texts on the same topic and then came together to consider ways to use them at different levels in classrooms.

Professional Reading Study Group

Study group members can choose to read one professional text on a topic or multiple texts on a topic. Whereas some teachers try out new practices by staying close to the texts they are reading, others adapt the practices they read about to fit the needs of their particular classrooms. Conversations around the professional books lead to lively and engaging inquiry. Kim Prettyman found that the teachers in her building especially enjoyed meeting with teachers from different grade levels they didn't usually get to see. Teachers in her study group also enjoyed it when the texts they were discussing confirmed their current instructional practices. "Sometimes teachers were confirmed by what they were reading, as it matched or was similar to what they were already doing," she said.

Getting Study Groups Started

To get started, I listen to teachers and together we decide on a topic of interest. Teachers are motivated when I follow their lead and address the issues they consider paramount to their teaching and learning. Some teachers want to focus on issues they are struggling with in their classrooms, whereas others want to delve more deeply into areas where they are more confident. To select texts, I ask myself what teachers are ready for and interested in. Would readings that are more practical or more conceptual be most beneficial? Will everyone read the same text? Will there be different texts on similar topics?

Once texts are selected, we can decide if we want to read chapter by chapter, section by section, topic by topic, or read the entire text and then have a discussion. It is important to consider time constraints. How often will we meet? Can more than one study group be held at the same time? Dates might not work out for some individuals, and other teachers might prefer different texts.

Engaging in Schoolwide Study Groups

Kim Prettyman surveyed the classroom teachers and principal in her building to begin schoolwide study groups. Based upon their interests, she clustered the teachers into five study groups. She selected professional books for each group, and teachers chose how much they would read before each meeting.

Kim held her study groups during every other faculty meeting. "The agreement with the principal was to have every other faculty meeting dedicated to book groups," she said. "For the first five to ten minutes we met as a faculty to share what was happening in our groups—what we had tried in the classroom, what worked, what didn't. Then we broke into our five groups for the remaining hour. Each group chose a leader and a note taker and decided where they would meet each time. Most teachers met in the classrooms of one of the group members and read a chapter or two every two weeks."

Initial interest was high. "After the first several book club meetings teachers were very excited. Teachers were thanking me for the time to read a professional text and have the opportunity to digest it with someone else."

The plan for the study groups worked elegantly on paper, but Kim encountered several unanticipated glitches along the way. "Scheduling conflicts occurred, and professional faculty meetings turned into business meetings," she said. "The time allotted at faculty meetings dwindled to ten to twenty minutes instead of the full hour promised. This was frustrating to teachers who were expected to have a meaningful conversation long after their expected ending time." Kim also learned that the groups needed more scaffolding. Initially she joined one study group. Although this worked well for her particular group, other groups had a harder time getting started and maintaining interest and motivation. So, in addition to facilitating whole-group conversations and being a member of just one group, Kim came to see the importance of moving in and out of groups to learn what topics and issues they were raising and exploring.

Kim encountered three administrative changes as well. "All were very supportive of the idea, and the involvement of each was very different. The first principal gave his approval and provided professional money for the books to be purchased. Then he left that summer. The second principal joined a group and became very involved with that group and left the other groups on their own. The third principal surveyed the teachers about the groups. During one faculty meeting each group gave a summary of the main ideas and concepts learned from each book. Then the schoolwide professional development took a new direction."

Lessons Learned

As Kim noted, "For study groups to really work, time needs to be spent beyond the school day and allotted by administration. Teachers need to be invested in their own learning and professional development. In study groups, teachers can try out what they are learning in their professional text and then have the safety to discuss that in their groups. Learning is messy, and study groups help teachers let go of the false notion that they have to get it perfect the first time. The greatest growth occurs when there is freedom to try a researched practice, reflect individually, reflect with other professionals, and then make changes together."

As collaborative endeavors, study groups support and extend teachers' interests and learning. Together, teachers come to see themselves as knowers as they share their learning and consider new possibilities for implementing instructional practices. As Kim reminds us, study groups do not happen without sustained intent.

TOOL 10: TRANSCRIBING LESSONS AND CONFERRING WITH TEACHERS

I have been transcribing lessons since I observed student teachers at an undergraduate institution. It is an instructional tool I continue to use today. The predictable format of each conference and the accompanying transcription provide a framework for powerful reflections and discussions around lessons.

In Practice

Janet invited me into her fifth-grade classroom to observe her first modeled writing lesson during writer's workshop. For this lesson she chose to write about when she was trapped in an elevator as a young child. As we walked to the faculty room after the observation, Janet talked about the experience of writing in front of her class.

> **Cheryl:** What went well?
>
> **Janet:** They [the students] generated lots of good questions. They take it seriously. They care and they really want to help you [as a writer]. This was my first time sharing a piece of my writing, and it felt good to do that.

As the conversation continued, we then turned our attention to the transcription of the lesson to examine the details of the classroom conversation. We pointed to particular comments made by the students and how Janet responded to their queries. The transcription provided a foundation for our conversation.

> **Janet:** What questions do you have [about the piece of writing]?
>
> **Student:** How long did it take before you got united?
>
> **Student:** Was it scary?
>
> **Student:** Was this a parking garage?

Student: I think it sounds good just as it is. It keeps you wondering.

Student: Why didn't your mother tell you to wake up?

Janet: Well, my mother and I have talked about this, now that I am older. It seemed like a long time, but it wasn't really. It's helping me to share this with you. When you're stuck on a piece of writing, what do you do?

Student: Ask people around me.

Student: Were you scared to go in the elevators again?

Janet: Even now I won't go in an elevator by myself.

Student: It made me think you were in a mall.

Janet: Oh, it was a parking garage in a hotel.

Student: Add that you were in Washington, D.C. Was it a fancy elevator? Was it a new elevator?

Janet: So, you think I need to add more about where the elevator is, what kind of elevator, and add more [details]. Thanks.

Framework

Transcribing

Before each observation, I ask teachers what they would like me to attend to during the observation. In this way, the teacher leads the observation. When transcribing a teacher's lessons, I include discussions generated during the lesson. I transcribe conversations, questions asked, student responses, and the nature of the interactions. Just as we ask teachers to follow the students' leads as learners, I work as a coach to follow the lead of the teacher.

The Conference Begins

After the lesson, the teachers and I follow a predictable structure to begin our conversations. I ask, "What went well?" and "What changes would you make to the lesson?" Everything starts from a known—what went well. Listening to what teachers believe went well and what changes they would consider making to their instruction offers me ways into the conversations by giving me a window into the learners' zones.

Initially, when teachers are trying to articulate what went well, I may "name" the literate behaviors for them. "I noticed you encouraged your students to read fluently." "Did you notice how you supported your students to self-correct?" "Several of your students made text-to-life connections during your lesson." At first, teachers may not be used to these conversations, so noticing and naming literate behaviors or instructional decision-making is not always easy. Therefore, together we name the literate behaviors that occur during the lesson.

The conversations provide a predictable framework where teachers anticipate the conversation and then articulate their instructional decisions and decision-making. As Janet commented,

I think the predictability of it was nice. …I knew what to expect. I could be thinking about what I'm going to say about it [the lesson]. For me, talking is very much a part of learning. I need to discuss things to gain from them and then go away and think about it.…To me, if you're going to just teach and not think about what happened, you're not going to learn anything. You should really be assessing and evaluating and thinking about what just went on, what just happened [in the lesson].

Turning to the Transcript

Next, the teachers and I focus specifically on the transcripts. The transcripts of the lessons provide a textual anchor for reflections, conversations, and future lesson planning. Here, I select one or two productive places to discuss. Otherwise, it would become overwhelming for everyone involved. The "nudges" are designed to move teachers forward. I am mindful to tell the teachers, up front, that I will be "nudging" them, and that this may cause some intellectual unrest and discomfort. Again, these choices are based on the teachers' expressed needs and interests, as well as on what I have noticed.

Together, the teachers and I add to the transcripts. To do this, I place the transcript squarely between the two of us so either the teacher or I can write on the paper. Generally, I write my suggestions under the heading "Ideas to Consider." These suggestions have included the following: "Notice what the other students are doing while you are reading with your guided reading group." "Let's think about the pacing of the lesson." "Let's look at ways students can locate information in the text while others are finishing their silent reading." "How much time are the students reading connected text? Is this the same for all of your students?"

Teachers routinely tell me that they revisit their transcripts and use them to design future lessons. Janet noted, "One of the nice things about having everything written down was that moments that you might have missed inadvertently, you could go back and say, 'Wow, look at what so-and-so said; that was such an interesting thing.' I could go back to it [the transcript] a few days later in the classroom if I wanted to, or make a comment to a student."

Given that the scripts are learning spaces for the teachers, they are intended solely for the teachers' reflections. Teachers choose whether or not to share them with administrators or with other teachers.

Independent Scripting

The conversations and accompanying transcriptions also provide models for teachers to use independently to observe one another. Once teachers see the value of transcribing lessons, many invite colleagues into their classrooms to observe. Together, they theorize about the lesson and the responses of the students. Just last week I heard, "I never thought to use that book for introducing setting. That worked out really well." "Wow, I really liked the way you organized your independent reading. I want to try that. The students were so engaged."

The following example illustrates another way teachers support and respond to one another when observing. In this example, Sue observed Gail working one on one with Tim, a reluctant reader in fourth grade. Because Tim often tried to avoid reading texts, Gail asked Sue to focus on the range of ways she supported Tim as a reader.

This was the first time Sue observed another teacher, and she was concerned about transcribing a lesson. Though she didn't transcribe it verbatim, the notations Sue gave to Gail captured many of the instructional interactions. Sue offers positive, productive, and specific feedback to her colleague.

Gail and Tim
11-6-03

Your prompts:
- *Tell me what's happening in the picture.*
- *That word is tricky.*

Getting ready to read:
- *Tim was engaged after your book introduction.*
- *Level of support. You asked, "How did you know?"*
- *You asked Tim, "What's flipping?" (Here you're the learner.)*

Your introduction was very detailed to support his comprehension. His book was Guided Reading Level J. (He's in fourth grade.)
- *Tim's connection to text—"I'd get suspended."*
- *Tim was very engaged. He showed excitement about the book.*
- *Your response, "You knew!"—very encouraging.*
- *Tim read with expression.*

I noticed:

- *You were very relaxed and work well together. Very encouraging. You let him do the work.*

Connection to my teaching:

I have been practicing wait time. You give him a lot of time.

TOOL 11: VISITING COLLEAGUES' CLASSROOMS

Classroom visitations are another tool for building teachers' self-extending systems. These visits are an opportunity for a collaborative exchange to gain ideas and insights about teaching and learning—how teachers teach, how children learn, and how children engage in learning opportunities. As we notice and name strategic learning for students, we want to notice and name our instructional practices. Watching each other helps us become more astute observers of literacy, literacy development, and instructional practices. Together we have an opportunity to name our teaching decisions, our teaching moves, and our teaching practices. During the conversations we can see commonalities, differences, language choices we can appropriate, and multiple practices to incorporate into our classrooms to extend our teaching repertoire.

The conversations and the lesson transcriptions provide an analytic space in which to theorize with colleagues about different teaching styles. The scripting and conversation provide a detailed analysis of the teaching moves and the ways the students engage in the learning during a lesson. This analysis provides a framework with which to move beyond impressionistic observations such as, "The lesson went well." "It was dreadful." "The lesson worked out nicely."

The following vignette, written by Linda Shekita, details a thirty-minute observation lesson with two second-grade students in the reading room. Three teachers observed this writing lesson.

I Waited, and I Waited, and I Waited: Building Thoughts in Silences

Beth and John entered the reading room and joined me at the small round table. I had placed several previously read books on the table as models of writing possibilities. Beth and John walked into my classroom that afternoon knowing they were going to write. I planned to support them if they needed ideas for a new piece of writing.

When I asked if John or Beth already had a topic in mind, John quickly offered, "I might do a mixture— I might combine two books. I might use Victor."

John's response surprised and confused me. Previously, he had written personal narratives, responses to literature, or nonfiction responses. I quickly turned around to select several more Victor books from the bookshelf behind the writing table.

"Wow, John. If you decide to write fiction today, you'll need to think about where the piece takes place, the problem, and the characters. You think about that and decide. You're the author." Beth, meanwhile, shared that she wanted to write about playing basketball on Saturday. I told them both, "It's up to you. Think about how you're going to plan your pieces. You can plan by sketching pictures, by putting down some words you want to include, or by thinking about your pieces."

I placed a writing toolbox containing pens (red, black, blue), pencils (fancy and regular), scissors, highlighter, glue, date stamp, black marker, white-out tape, and erasers on the table and reminded them, "Get your tools when you're ready."

John decided to create his own book based on a character from the Victor series that also included features found in the Mercer Mayer book Just Me and My Puppy. *When I asked him how he planned to organize his piece, he said, "I'll use mind pictures."*

I then turned my attention to Beth, who hadn't yet started her piece of writing. "Is there anything I can help you with?"

"I think all I have to do is be quiet and think," she said.

Then, I waited, and I waited, and I waited.

After several minutes, I started to prompt Beth about her basketball game. "Can you tell me what happened?"

"At first, I was nervous. When I took my first shot, I was happy." As Beth continued to talk, I wrote the following words on a Post-it: cheer, clap, coach, basketball.

At this point in our thirty-minute lesson, Beth still hadn't written anything.

I prompted, "What tool are you going to use today?"

"I have to think about that."

Again, I waited.

"I think I'm going to use a pen today. Now for the color."

John was still writing his title in bubble letters. "John, you have one more minute to finish your title."

Beth finally began to write. As she wrote, "I went to basketball. I felt nervous," she looked up and exclaimed, "That basketball Post-it—wherever I need it, I move it there!"

John talked quietly as he wrote, rereading his entire piece after every few words. After a bit, he looked up to ask, "Is a *a capital letter when it is alone?"*

"Look in the book," I replied.

As Beth and John wrote, I wrote along with them about my son, Will. During our thirty-minute lesson, all of the observers wrote, too.

> *Beth continued to write: "Once I got a shot I felt happy."*
>
> *"Beth, your words are painting the picture of your basketball game."*
>
> *–Linda Shekita*

The lesson ended as Beth, John, and Linda shared their writing. During this lesson, Linda gave both Beth and John (and herself) the space to plan and to write. Drawing bubble letters was rehearsal for John. Quiet thinking time provided Beth's rehearsal space. Together, they built thoughts within the silences. Because Linda wrote, too, she gave her students the space to write independently. She gave them the time and the tools to do the hard work of writing and to develop their self-extending systems as writers.

During our follow-up conversation, when discussing what went well, Linda noted that both students engaged in writing. She commented that the silence felt even bigger while she was observed. Because of the observation, she was more aware of the amount of silence and wait time she gave her writers.

This observation was a place for all of us to examine what we think writing work and the work of writers looks like. The silence during the lesson was, at times, painful. There was no catchy lesson or chatting to take up the space. Beth needed silence (on this day), and John readily embraced the props provided. Beth named her needs as a writer. John named his needs as a writer. Linda followed their leads as learners.

During the conversation after the lesson, we moved beyond our initial thoughts and impressions of the lesson—the slow pace, the silences, the seeming avoidance of the writers—to note the specificity with which Linda followed the lead of the learners, honored their need for silence, and still nudged them to continue writing. By the end of the thirty minutes, John had written seventy-one words of his first fiction piece...and there have been many more since.

Focusing on Strengths

Each conversation after an observation begins with
something that went well during the lesson. We have
discussed effective strategies, ways a student took up a
prompt, the conversational nature of lessons, connections
students made to texts, and ways children experimented with
language during writing. Starting with strengths provides
an anchor for the conversation. As one teacher said, "After
naming all the things that went well, and hearing from others
what I did well, I was ready for a nudge." This comment was
highly instructive for me as a coach. It led me to wonder,
When are we ready for nudges? How do we create a trusting
environment so people are willing to open their doors and
invite others in to observe?

Nudging and Extending the Repertoire

After listening to the observed teacher talk about what
went well during the lesson, we focus on the transcription.
During observations, some teachers focus their attention on
the learners and transcribe how they engage in the lesson,
whereas other observers focus on the teachers and transcribe
the language that accompanies the instructional decisions.
See Appendix B, which is designed to provide a shared
language for teachers.

The transcription of the lesson provides multiple points
of view for the conversation and grounds it in the language
of the lesson. During one book introduction for guided
reading, the teacher asked five questions in a row before
giving her students an opportunity to respond. She was
surprised to learn this as we analyzed the script. She had not
realized she did this so extensively and decided she would
be mindful of it in future lessons. Another teacher noted that
she would introduce vocabulary words in context in her next
lesson, because her students had such difficulty reading the
words she previewed on a whiteboard before the lesson.

Reflecting

The conversation ends with the questions, "What did you learn? What are you thinking?" Everyone participates. Comments have included the following: "After watching this lesson, I'm less nervous about starting poetry in my room. I got so many ideas for how to begin. I also liked how you named your students as poets." "I noticed how detailed your book introductions were. I need to go back and look at mine and see how I can make them stronger." "I liked how you used a range of prompts. I need to use more prompts during my lessons." "I liked how you just focused on revision during the conference. I try to do too much when I confer."

To Consider

Teachers can visit classrooms in the same building, at different grade levels, and to help children make the transition from one school to another. In my experience, teachers benefit more from observing classrooms in their own building or district. This avoids the "not like my students" syndrome. When I have set up observations in other schools, teachers haven't gained as much as they do when they collaborate with teachers in their own building or district.

Classroom visitations can be highly instructive. They can also create tension and discord, especially if teachers are not used to observing one another. Until trust develops, you can expect intellectual unrest. As teachers observe their colleagues, know the history of the building where you are working. Some teachers may have histories that prevent them from wanting to work together. It is especially important to notice and name the issues that arise and problem-solve together. As we routinely ask children to work together, visiting colleagues' classrooms offers a way for children to see teachers working together.

TOOL 12: EXTENDING THE LEARNING COMMUNITY: SHARING KNOWLEDGE

The final tool is open ended. You and the teachers you work with might choose to present at local, statewide, and national conferences and workshops; teach courses; guest lecture; or write journal articles, chapters, or books. This is your space to share the insights you have gained in your coaching experiences with others. In developing self-extending systems, our collective work becomes generative.

In the following vignette, Rose, a second-grade teacher, and Mindy, the school librarian, collaborated to develop a professional growth plan. Given the emphasis in their building on improving writing instruction and writing development, they selected and cataloged a range of mentor texts classroom teachers could use for writer's workshop. Together, they identified potential authors, read widely, and then chose books that exemplified craft features taught during writer's workshop. Once a book was selected, the craft feature was included in its bibliographic record. As a result of this newly developed coding system, teachers can easily search the school's online library catalog for specific craft features they want to teach.

Finding Common Ground: A Professional Development Plan Evolves

It was an exciting time in our building. The teachers were invested in writing instruction and were using Craft Lessons *by Ralph Fletcher and JoAnn Portalupi and Lucy Calkins's* Units of Study for Primary Writing *to generate ideas for writer's workshop. The reading teacher and building principal suggested that the recommended books in these texts be given more accessible subject headings in the school library's online catalog. When Rose, a second-*

grade teacher, heard about the plan, she approached me [Mindy] to collaborate on the project. Because Rose enjoyed using children's literature in her daily teaching, she had ideas about extending the original plan. With Craft Lessons *and* Units of Study *as guides, we decided to learn more about mentor texts and generate additional titles. Instead of simply inputting the existing titles, we decided to research other texts that could be used to introduce craft features during mini-lessons.*

We jumped at the opportunity to collaborate to produce a living resource of titles that complemented the reading and writing instruction in the building. It was an exciting challenge. We both thought that having the chance to create a professional development plan like this one really gave us the opportunity to grow as teachers and continue to be lifelong learners. We invited a first-grade teacher to participate in the project to broaden the range of perspective.

Once we had our idea in place, the toughest part of the project was getting started. How would we choose books and authors? Which lesson topics would we focus on? It was quite overwhelming at first. We finally narrowed our craft features to great leads, endings both surprise and satisfying, dialogue, beginning/ middle/end, and transition words. Then we found authors our first and second graders would enjoy and studied their works. We started with Eric Carle, Kevin Henkes, Eileen Christelow, and Tomie dePaola. For the first year of this project, we limited ourselves to identifying authors with last names that start with A-L.

We each took a stack of books to read, made notes about them as we read, and then switched books with each other. Each Monday during the school year, we would meet to share, discuss, and compare our notes. We kept a printed list of the books we were reading, and the books we didn't select were crossed off.

We read more than 200 books and ultimately chose 50 to use for our project. We worked on the majority-of-two rule. Two of us needed to agree on how the book fit the criteria. We read aloud from the text the parts that showed proof of the intended lesson topic. Once a book was agreed upon, it was added to the list.

Once the list was finalized, local subject headings were added to the school's online catalog. This makes searching for a mentor text much easier. All a teacher needs to do is type in one of the targeted criteria, such as leads or endings, and a list of books becomes accessible. We were pleased to find so many books in our school library that met the criteria we had chosen. We even discovered new authors. For example, the author Lisa Campbell Ernst has many titles that are excellent to use for writing mini-lessons. Her stories offer a clear beginning, middle, and end; transition words; and satisfying endings. Before this project, she was not an author whose works teachers often read.

One afternoon while we were working on the project, we discussed our process with Cheryl. As we all talked, we saw how this professional development plan connected with Cheryl's master's-level writing class at UAlbany. After our conversation, Cheryl invited us to speak to her graduate writing class. Students in her class were completing a mentor text assignment as part of the course. We spent the evening talking with the graduate students about our professional development project and our excitement about mentor texts. During the class, we broke into small groups and shared our findings. We noticed that we all used certain authors for our mentor text lessons. The evening was a rich exchange of ideas. There were many people in that room—all teachers teaching each other the value of great literature and giving the gift of sharing ideas, an experience that teachers do not often seem to have enough time to do. We were very glad for

this opportunity to talk about our plan and learn from many other teachers.
    –Mindy Grey and Rose Wilson

This chapter on building self-extending systems has included the voices of many teachers. When teachers inquire and learn together, they collaboratively construct new understandings. As we listen to one another, challenge one another, and analyze our teaching and learning, we, like our students, clarify and extend our understandings.

Coaches also help teachers identify opportunities to transfer their learning to new situations. When teachers' self-extending systems are operating, the learning is generative as they discover, question, wonder, challenge, and create opportunities for continued and sustained growth. The chapter begins in a second-grade classroom as Lora supported her students to become independent researchers and ends with Nancy Werner's kindergartners changing policy at their local public library.

Democracy in Action

The journey began when I wrote my February monthly newsletter for my kindergarten classroom. We were in the midst of a reading and writing celebration called PARP, "People as Reading Partners," and students were encouraged to go to the public library to get library cards and books so that they could be reading every day.

A week later Michael entered the classroom and said, "We went to the library and they told me kindergartners can't have library cards."

At circle time that day, I wanted to check to see if anyone else had had a similar experience. I learned that a few of the other students had also tried to get library cards but couldn't. I said, "It sounds like the library has a rule that kindergartners aren't allowed to get library cards. Do you think that's fair?"

After a humming of conversations and comments that included, "No, that's not fair," I continued. "Why do you think they would make a rule like that?"

"Maybe they think we're too little."

"Maybe they think we'll rip their books."

"Maybe they think we can't read."

"I originally thought Michael should write the library a letter, but since this issue affects us all, maybe we should work together on it."

The class responded with a chorus of "Yeah!"

So, with marker in hand and chart paper ready, I started our joint letter:

To the Public Library,

We are kindergartners. We want to get library cards. We don't think it's fair that we have to wait until first grade.

I asked, "What can we say in our letter so they know we are responsible enough for library cards?"

We won't lose the library card. We will take care of it. Don't worry! We will keep it safe. We will take care of our books. We won't rip the card. We will keep our books in a safe place. We are learning how to read, and books help us.

Can you please let us have library cards in kindergarten?

Each child signed the letter. Then Michael raised his hand. "So, can we take it over there right now?" Although I admired his persistence, I explained that I couldn't take them on a field trip without permission. I told the class that I would drop off the letter at the mailbox and that I hoped the librarian would write back. I then shared our letter with the principal and school librarian.

When I called the library, I said I was a kindergarten teacher and asked the librarian to explain the library card policy. I told her that my student Michael had been denied a card when he went to the library. I learned that children could get library cards in June before they entered first grade. The librarian explained that the policy worked well for the library because it brought families in for summer programs.

When I asked why students couldn't have the cards earlier, the librarian talked about lost cards and five-dollar fees, young children who take out too many books, and parents who use a child's library card when they have misused their own. I then mentioned the letter my students had written to the library and made it clear that although the letter was their idea and their words, I supported their position. I shared that kindergartners learn in our school library how to be responsible and to take care of books. At the beginning of kindergarten, families establish new routines that include reading for homework and perhaps visiting their library.

I asked if she would mind if we walked to the library to deliver the letter. She was gracious and welcoming, but she was not in charge of policy-making. The decision rested with the library board.

As children and parents walked past local businesses to the library to deliver the letter, I explained that it might be hard to persuade grown-ups to change rules. I gave Michael the letter and his fingers gripped the giant paper. When we opened the door, crowds of adults were in the little room. Our principal was smiling ear to ear, along with the district assistant superintendent, the town supervisor, and several library board members.

Michael handed the librarian the letter. Our words were there, right there, for the world to see. When she asked if somebody would like to read it, my entire class read the letter together. The library board president explained to the children that to change a rule, everybody in charge of the library had to agree and vote on it. She said that just like we have a principal to help make decisions in our school, she had to talk to the people in charge of the library to decide. At that moment, a small group of adults moved into another room, letter in hand, to take a vote. Silence followed their departure.

The board members reappeared after their deliberation and said, "We've considered your proposal. What we've decided to do is to let anyone who has participated in the PARP program have a library card." It took a moment for the children to realize what they had just accomplished. Cheers and claps erupted from the crowd. Our words mattered.

–Nancy Werner

06 Broadening the Coaching Role: Developing Partnerships with Administrators and Engaging with Families

Although literacy coaches work primarily with teachers, successful literacy coaching includes the broader school community as well. In this chapter, I invite administrators to consider their role in developing successful partnerships with literacy coaches. Later in the chapter I explore ways coaches can support teachers to engage with and learn from families.

BUILDING RELATIONSHIPS WITH ADMINISTRATORS

We bring our understandings of coaching to each meeting, to each conversation, and to each encounter, and must continuously navigate those understandings. It is important to have conversations early and often with administrators (principals, instructional supervisors, assistant superintendents, and superintendents) to discuss expectations and responsibilities. Together, we can determine how best to keep administrators informed. I have worked with administrators who want to approve agendas for meetings, and others who join workshops and experience the unfolding of the agenda side by side with the teachers. It depends on the administrator, and it is important to find each one's preferences. In this way, we can make sure we are on the same page (or at the very least a similar page). The International Reading Association addresses the central role of administrators in successful literacy coaching: "If reading coaches are to be successful in promoting changes in classroom practices, the expectations for the role of the reading coach need to be clear and understood by both the reading coaches and the school administrator, in addition to being supported by the school administrator" (2004, 3).

Administrators influence the literacy content coaches provide and the ways coaches engage with teachers. Administrators can also provide or deny access—to resources, time, and instructional practices. To work together, coaches and administrators each need to discuss how they envision the coach's role. How does your administrator envision your role? What responsibilities will you be given? How much autonomy do you have as a coach? How do you negotiate these perspectives? What if there are varying and competing perspectives? What happens if there is a philosophical mismatch? As Toll (2005) cautions, "While you are busy developing trust, engaging in dialogue, listening and learning, your principal may think you should be telling, monitoring, and correcting" (33). In Peggy O'Shea's district there was a good match. Peggy, an assistant superintendent, commented on how much she gained from listening to the teachers celebrate each time they met together. "In the beginning, when you go around and talk about what is working, what is going well, this leads to more than a sharing of ideas. It brings together teachers from three different schools. There's lots of cross pollinating. When you model and then discuss what has just happened, you are very open in terms of communication. We're finding our strengths and using each other's strengths."

This is in direct contrast to a principal who told me, "Don't spend so much time sharing what is going well in classrooms. The teachers need to learn content. You need to train them." Clearly, I did not articulate my goals and purposes well enough, because this comment was made several times. This principal later chose a scripted writing program for her teachers because she thought I did not "train" the teachers quickly enough. For this particular administrator, I should have been far more explicit about the importance of constructing meaning through instructional conversations and collaborative inquiry.

Not all principals or administrators bring strong understandings of literacy and literacy development to their positions. I appreciate when principals or administrators are clear to their teachers that there are certain literacy practices or aspects of literacy development that they want (or need) to learn more about. I most appreciate when administrators say this up front and position themselves as learners. Principals and assistant superintendents have said, "I have a secondary background. What do I need to know to best support my teachers?" "In my past jobs I never had to do running records. Help me learn more about them." "What should the class look like when the students are engaged in writer's workshop? It seems so noisy, yet they're writing." "How can I help the teachers manage the rest of the class when the teachers have guided reading groups?" "What professional readings will help me understand what my teachers are doing and learning about?" These questions set up an inquiry space that transfers to buildings. In these buildings, we learn collaboratively.

I invite administrators to become part of every learning experience during workshops or grade-level meetings. If we're scoring and analyzing running records, analyzing writing samples, or sketching or responding to texts, I want the administrators, like the teachers, to experience what it means to be a learner. Many have commented, "I'd forgotten how hard it is to keep up with running records." Others, like the teachers, note which literacy events they prefer. When we are all positioned as learners, we converse learner to learner. As Hawley and Valli (1999) remind us, "Effective professional development involves continuous teacher and administrator learning in the context of collaborative problem solving. When professional development is thought of as a program or a series of formal scheduled events, or is otherwise disconnected from authentic problem solving, it is unlikely to have much influence on teacher and student learning" (144).

One principal, Micah Brown, noted, "I can't even imagine not attending the sessions. I've grown as a professional in my own learning and knowing. Attending helped me form a bond with my staff. Now my role is not evaluating and judging. We have a common language and bond. We're reading the same books; we have the same references." Understanding literacy, literacy development, and literacy practices takes time. Teachers walk the path at different times and in different ways, just as students engage in their own ways (Clay 1998). When administrators engage as learners, they can better understand the ebbs and flows of learning. By attending sessions with their teachers and engaging as learners, administrators send a powerful message that learning is collaborative. These situations reduce power differentials and hierarchies when everyone contributes to the conversation.

FOCUSING ON TEACHERS' PROFESSIONAL GROWTH AND DEVELOPMENT

Micah, a building principal for four years, offers several ways she follows her teachers' leads to support their professional growth and development. First, she advocates for literacy coaching. "When I got here, I saw how excited the teachers were. I've worked to continue the long-term coaching relationship that existed before I arrived." Second, she listens to what is important to her teachers and becomes part of the learning community. "Teachers ask me in to talk about instruction and to see what they're working on in their classrooms—it might be the questions they're asking or the prompts they're using. They'll say, 'Take a look, this is what I'm working on.' Teachers also invite me to their publishing parties. I know how important they are, so I try not to miss them." Third, she maintains a schedule for uninterrupted time for reading and writing. "That has been a challenge because of specials and other considerations. It is an easy thing to disintegrate if you are not committed to that." Fourth, she reads books recommended by her teachers. "The teachers suggest books for me to read, both children's books and professional books. My librarian is a great resource. She introduces me to genres that she is excited about and interested in." Fifth, Micah unifies her building to support all learners. "I make sure that reading support [academic intervention] is seen as an integral part of the school, not isolated. I also make sure that special education and pupil services staff are on board. They can come from a deficit model, and that is not allowed. They participate in the same professional development. When they walk into classrooms, they know what to do."

Similarly, Peggy O'Shea asks her teachers about their specific professional development needs. She begins conversations with what is working and what is not. "We've springboarded from that with books and materials. The teachers are very comfortable talking about their needs. We work together to set them up for what they need and what would assist them."

TIMING MATTERS

Several years ago, I was invited to an exploratory meeting with a small group of teachers, a principal, and an assistant superintendent. As I listened to their expectations for professional development, the assistant superintendent shared that there was not a coherent literacy program in place, and he wanted district test scores raised immediately.

During the conversation, I learned he primarily wanted professional development that emphasized a "quick fix." After listening, I concluded that I wasn't the right match for the district at that time. I offered that if the teachers and administrators wanted to consider a more expansive view of literacy and literacy instruction, I would be happy to speak with them to see if our needs and interests matched.

Indeed, three years later, with a new administration in place, I was hired to work with this district for several years. The change in administration led to a change in the district's view of literacy development and literacy instruction. Together with the teachers I developed a long-range literacy plan for the district that involved extensive modeling of instructional practices, incorporating literacy blocks into the curriculum, developing a guided reading book room, advocating for a larger repertoire of literacy materials, facilitating workshops during school and after school, and engaging families. Over time, we examined and reexamined literacy practices, assessments used, and interventions provided. These conversations led to the redesign of the report cards in the elementary school.

Not all administrators will join your sessions. Not all administrators will be open about their knowledge of (or gaps in) literacy and literacy development. Some administrators will become unnerved if they see their teachers taking on an agentive role and questioning long-held practices in the school/district. These are moments where coaches need to step back and analyze the landscape. Sometimes, coaches need to adapt, adjusting to the needs of the particular context. I have had administrators leave sessions just as we were getting ready to respond to literature or engage in difficult conversations about the alignment between report cards and assessments. Once, a principal left just as we were about to score and analyze running records. He returned once the conversation was finished—even though administering and analyzing running records were the very issues his teachers were grappling with. After this happened, I made it a point to rework the agenda so that difficult issues were discussed and addressed when the administrator was present.

REFLECTIONS FOR ADMINISTRATORS

When coaches work with teachers, there will be changes on conceptual, financial, and practical levels. As an administrator, are you ready for the changes that will occur in your building or district? As teachers become more knowledgeable about literacy development and literacy practices, they will need additional resources—for their students and for their own professional growth and development. In one instance, as teachers moved to guided reading groups, they needed leveled texts. We started small and shared an initial pool of books. Over time I helped teachers pick favorite authors, favorite series, and a range of genres to stock their developing book rooms. As we purchased new materials, we were careful to look for gaps in the existing materials. We also purchased a range of professional resource materials for teachers. When I introduced books on guided reading, comprehension, writer's workshop, conferring with writers, and strategy instruction, we made sure there were copies in the professional development libraries. Although some books were purchased for the entire staff, we came to discover that buying fewer books increased the number of conversations. Teachers shared books with one another, complete with highlights, margin notes, and Post-its.

For administrators, there are scheduling considerations as well. When and how will coaches work with teachers? What time of year is more beneficial for teachers? What opportunities are available over time? What will a coach's day look like? How does this change over time, during testing? Are meetings scheduled before school, during school, after school? Will there be a combination of mandated meetings and invitational meetings?

As an administrator, how will you support and sustain the climate of inquiry created in your building or district? Personnel will change. Coaches may leave, or funding may dry up. However, once the tools have become internalized, they become part of the culture of the school. You can continue to meet together, begin each session with celebrations, provide coverage for collaborative observations, examine student work, and develop study groups. The tools outlined in this book can be used to promote and sustain ongoing inquiry, even if (or when) a coach leaves. New teachers joining the building can be apprenticed into a collaborative community just as children are. Once children self-correct as readers and understand when and how to self-correct, it doesn't matter if they read with their teachers, with their families, or independently—their self-extending systems are in place.

FAMILY ENGAGEMENT: LEARNING FROM FAMILIES

As a coach, I encourage teachers to learn from families to support children as learners, thinkers, and knowers. Insights gained from families bring forth the complexities of our learners and ensure that we think and act more broadly and deeply to bridge literacy, literacy instruction, and literacy competencies beyond school walls. One of my goals is to help teachers consider how they engage with families (Compton-Lilly 2003). The family-school connections discussed in this chapter started in the university literacy lab and then transferred to classrooms in unique ways.

INVITING FAMILIES INTO CLASSROOMS

As you might guess, I enjoy participating in my own children's classrooms. I much prefer when I am asked to listen to children read or to confer with young writers, but I have also cut my fair share of pumpkins, ghosts, and candy canes for class projects! Some teachers ask for my preferences, whereas others routinely assign "housekeeping" duties. Although I prefer working directly with children, other parents do not have schedules that permit them to spend time in the classrooms. They offer to help out in other ways, such as organizing art projects at home. Each family brings strengths and expertise.

Questions I routinely ask teachers include the following: When we invite parents into our classrooms, what is our goal, and what is our purpose? Do we offer a range of ways for families to participate? How can we welcome families to participate in ways that work for them? Are families there to help decorate the classroom? To organize art or cooking projects? Are they there to read one on one with children? Provide an audience for young writers? Do we only look for parents to assist with field trips and come to presentations, or is family involvement an ongoing, integral event in our classroom worlds? What do we learn when we invite families into our classrooms? How does what we learn from families matter in our instructional practices?

In the literacy lab, we invite families to observe their children during the tutorial. Siblings are always welcome. During this time, we learn from and with families. When tutors and families talk together, they discover how to better support the children's learning at home and in school. Parents often tell us in the literacy lab that some of the prompts we use during the sessions are new to them. They find that our instructional language is quite different, and they like seeing how their children respond. These conversations with parents led us to create bookmarks to develop a shared language for reading and writing prompts. To promote shared language with families, I encourage teachers to create their own bookmarks to send home.

We've heard parents say they could not believe how engaged their children were during lessons at the lab. They noted that when they worked with their children at home, it could be like "pulling teeth" to get them to read. This led to conversations about the types of books available for children at home. We learned that some of the books were too difficult for the children, even books with "Easy Reader" labels. These insights helped all of us pay more attention to text features and text demands. At the end of the semester, tutors give books to the children that they can read successfully, along with an additional list of accessible texts. This experience helped me rethink the purposes for the books we send home with students. Now when I work with teachers as a coach, I ask, Are we clearly delineating ways books can be read and shared with families? To help families support their children, when children bring books home, teachers can select (or have the children select) laminated tags that say, "I can read this book to you," "I can read this book with you," or "Let's read this book together."

One tutor in the lab discovered that her approach was far too relaxed during her lessons after watching her student engage with his mother. When the tutor appropriated the parent's language, she worked more successfully with her student. This tutor also discovered that she had been offering too much choice. She learned from the child's mother that choice within parameters was more beneficial. Once the child saw his mother and tutor working together, he took his learning more seriously. This insight led me to encourage teachers to invite parents into their classrooms to observe and participate in lessons.

After I described multiple ways we engage with families in the literacy lab, Linda Shekita decided to invite families to visit her reading room. During visits, parents are encouraged to join and participate in the lessons. During their observations, parents talk about the different prompts the tutors use, comment on the amount of wait time, notice when their children self-correct, and comment on their children's levels of independence in reading and writing. They can see how their children engage with the books that are brought home each night in plastic bags to share with their families. As Linda listens to the parents and children, she seeks to hook them on books and favorite authors. At the earliest levels, it is always exciting to hear the students say, "I just read three Joy Cowley books, and this is my favorite." "I like books by Beverly Randall. Do you?" Each summer the children are sent home with individualized lists of guided reading leveled texts that they can take out of the local library.

In addition to reading room visits during the school year and prior to budget cuts that affected summer programs, the students were encouraged to take out books from the reading room in the summer. The reading room was open one day a week for parents to exchange books—books on the child's level that the child could read successfully. In these ways, Linda drew from family connections to motivate her students to transfer their literate competencies from the reading room to home. As a coach, I help teachers consider ways to invite families into their particular contexts in ways that matter to and work for families.

FAMILY JOURNALS

My work with family journals started in the literacy lab. To invite families to participate in family journals (Shockley, Michalove, and Allen 1995), teachers write a letter asking parents to share and discuss books with their children. In this letter, families are offered numerous possibilities for engaging in the journals, emphasizing that there is no right or wrong way to respond to the books read. The focus of the journal is on the time spent reading, discussing, and savoring books. Parents can sketch, write, have the children respond, or have the children illustrate what their parents have written. Parents can write in their first language, and children can read their parents' stories and responses. The goal is for families to respond in ways that work for them. For many parents, the journals become treasured keepsakes. As one parent said, "One day my son will love going back and looking at the stories written inside."

As a coach, it has been exciting to help teachers think about how they can incorporate family journals into their classrooms. Some teachers prefer to use journals once a week, and others engage with the families more frequently. I have helped teachers think about their language choices and consider the range of ways they respond to families in the journal. If teachers have difficulties with journals, our conversations center around what they are hoping to accomplish by using this instructional tool.

In one kindergarten when students started to draw lines in their journals, their teacher, Nancy, offered them multiple types of paper for the journals. The children then chose which journal they preferred. In the journals, teachers concentrate on literacy strengths and celebrations since its focus is literacy, not behavioral issues. Families are busy and may have a hard time responding. If this happens, I encourage teachers to invite other teachers, custodial staff, bus drivers, older siblings, and older students to participate with the children.

Coaches can support teachers to create literate spaces and to become open to ideas we have not yet recognized or realized. Susan Garnett (2006) did this as a reading teacher when she used family journals to explore family histories. Each interaction beyond the school walls offers a unique lens through which to extend our understanding of families. Children and families lead us to consider new possibilities.

PHOTOGRAPHING OUR LIVES

In our university literacy lab, we provide each child with a disposable camera (Dozier, Johnston, and Rogers 2006). The photographs are informative and enlightening as we discover each child's interests and world beyond the school walls. Children are encouraged to take pictures of their communities, people who interest them, and their lived lives (Orellana and Hernandez 1999). They then write about the photographs they have taken. Once teachers have seen the effect of the cameras in building connections with their students and their families, many incorporate them beyond the literacy lab walls into their classroom worlds. In moving beyond the one-on-one setting, some teachers have asked parent-teacher organizations to provide funds for securing individual cameras or developing film. In other schools, some families offer to develop the film. Other teachers send home digital cameras on a rotating basis. When students return the cameras, the pictures are downloaded onto classroom computers and then printed.

As a coach, I look for ways to help teachers incorporate children's funds of knowledge (Moll et al. 1992) into their classrooms. Engaging with and learning from families broadens our understandings of our students and their literate competencies.

07 Considering Assessment

RETHINKING INSTRUCTION: A COLLABORATIVE ANALYSIS
OF RUNNING RECORDS

When the primary teachers at Riverview Elementary
School (a pseudonym) were learning to use and incorporate
running records as an assessment tool in their classrooms,
several indicated that although they were comfortable
scoring the running records, they were not as confident with
their analysis. Given the teachers' concerns, we engaged in
a conversation to revisit the goals, purposes, and uses of
running records for day-to-day instruction. At the end of the
first year of implementation, the teachers brought samples of
running records to grade-level meetings to analyze their data.

As we looked at the running records across the grades,
we noticed that accuracy rates were consistently high—at
the independent level for most students. We also noticed that
although the teachers were (almost) exclusively circling

V for "visual errors," there were few, if any, self-corrections or repetitions on the running records. The accuracy rates of the running records did, at first glance, look like the students were reading at their independent levels, but they were overusing the visual cueing system.

As we looked at the errors the children made, we considered when they might lose the meaning of the text. We were concerned that the children were decoding words accurately but were not comprehending the texts they were reading. As the teachers examined patterns, they noticed which children used multiple cueing systems and which relied extensively on one cueing system. We also discovered that in some classes children did not self-correct and did not use repetition strategies. In these classrooms, we began to name those behaviors so the students could use them.

This led to conversations about the prompts teachers used to encourage children to become strategic readers. Many teachers then realized that they, too, relied too much on visual prompts when children came to difficult words. To help teachers move beyond this, we turned their attention to the prompt sheet in the text *Guided Reading* (Fountas and Pinnell 1996) to extend their repertoire of prompts. I asked teachers to highlight the prompts they routinely and most comfortably used in one color. Then I invited them to highlight in another color the prompts they were willing to try. In this way, they expanded and developed their repertoire of prompts.

These conversations led the teachers to write praise points and teaching points directly on the running records and to look for patterns—for individual children and across the class. To analyze prompt choices, I asked them to label the types of prompts (M for meaning, S for syntax, V for visual) they used during lessons. In doing this, teachers analyzed their "in the moment" teaching decisions. As they considered their prompts over time, teachers could slow the process and reflect on their pedagogical decision-making.

We then talked about the discussions the teachers led—

when the children were more engaged and less engaged. Some talked of conversations that felt like "pulling teeth" as they worked to help the children make connections to the text. These conversations led to a reconsideration of moving students up guided reading levels too rapidly. We then developed criteria for moving children to the next guided reading levels. The criteria, which continue to be developed and discussed, include comprehension, self-correction rate, balance of the cueing systems, fluency, accuracy rate, stamina, and writing.

Our collaborative analysis over the course of several years has led to more detailed and astute observations and analysis—for student achievement and for instructional practices. With the students in the forefront of our thinking, we engaged in a schoolwide analysis to reflect on and reexamine instructional and assessment practices. As we continue to revisit how running records inform our teaching, we deepen our understandings of student learning, assessment, and teaching. This reflective inquiry and analysis has led to more powerful and strategic teaching.

ASSESSING AND COACHING

Coaches play critical roles in helping teachers think about assessment and assessment practices across the school. Vogt and Shearer (2003) maintain, "Assessment and instruction should be inextricably linked in a recursive, ongoing, and dynamic way" (91). As coaches engage teachers in conversations about the purposes of and usefulness of assessments, Johnston (1997) asserts, "Assessment conversations that sustain inquiry and learning are very different from those that sustain blame, reward, and punishment" (3). Mindful that "the patterns and details a teacher notices are the central aspect of assessment" (67) coaches can help teachers notice patterns, details, and specificities of children's literate competencies and development. Just as teachers need detailed information about their learners, "assessment data informs the coaching you do" (Lyons and Pinnell 2001, 76). Lyons and Pinnell remind us, "Your goal is to be sure teachers have systematic ways of keeping examples of student work and recording evaluations. You also want their records to provide useful information rather than mechanical documentation" (84). In these ways, coaches can help teachers choose assessments that inform their instruction, not just monitor it.

Coaches may also be required to help select and administer standardized tests for their district. Walpole and McKenna (2004) say, "Ironically, America's preoccupation with testing may actually threaten achievement by causing us to devote too much time to test preparation. …And it does make sense for a literacy coach to lead the effort to revisit the school's policies concerning how this type of testing is conducted" (87). Coaches, teachers, and administrators can engage in conversations about how and why particular tests are chosen.

Assessment responsibilities vary depending on a coach's particular context. For some coaches, assessments and assessment procedures consume a great deal of time— scoring, administering, collecting, and reporting. For others, assessments do not take such extensive time and space. In your coaching context, consider the percentage of coaching responsibilities that involve assessment, recognizing that this may change over the course of the year. Most important, examine what you learn from the assessments that are used and how this informs instruction.

This chapter explores how coaches can help teachers consider assessment and assessment practices by recording student learning, engaging in side-by-side assessments, having teachers complete formal assessments, examining how student growth is represented through report cards, and assessing materials in the building. The chapter ends with the question, How will I know if I am making a difference as a coach?

RECORDING STUDENT LEARNING

In the classroom, I encourage teachers to record student learning throughout the day. When I teach or model guided reading lessons or confer with children, I take modified running records, record what a child says during the conversation, and note specific strategies a child uses while reading. I also note a "quotable quote" from each child during each lesson. In this way, I work to show teachers the importance of recording how children make sense of texts and their strategic knowing. When I confer with students during either writing or reading, I record their conversations as well as the praise point and teaching point I have selected.

When teachers are working with their guided reading groups, I sit side by side with them and take anecdotal information on the children as well. After the lesson, the teacher and I can compare the information we each noted. This helps us both see what we are privileging, and together we learn from the conversations that follow.

I also ask teachers to look for patterns over time. After they have taken notes for a couple of weeks, I ask them to step back and analyze their notations. What information are they recording? Are they recording information about content, strategies used, or mostly mechanics? Then, I ask them to consider how their notes inform their instruction. Prompts I use for these conversations include the following: What are you noticing? What are you writing? What literate competencies are you documenting? What are you missing?

For these notations to be useful and accessible, I encourage teachers to find ways for recording that work for them. Some teachers write notes for children on Post-its and then cluster the Post-its onto individually labeled sheets in a three-ring binder. Others write their notations on address labels and then peel these off onto separate sheets. Some teachers prefer to record notes directly onto their lesson plans. They can then look to see how individual children, as well as groups, are progressing. Teachers routinely bring their systems (as well as their attempted systems) to share when we meet together.

ASSESSING STUDENTS TOGETHER

As you read in Chapter 3, I often sit side by side with teachers to analyze student work. During these times we focus on the child's strengths and instructional needs while analyzing the details of the student's work. I also sit side by side with teachers to complete district assessments. When we complete the assessments, we discuss our results and compare our findings. Working with the teachers gives me an opportunity to walk through the entire assessment process. Together, we brainstorm ways to revise the procedures as necessary. As a result of these conversations, we have revised cumbersome language in directions, replaced books used for benchmarks, and eliminated assessments that did not provide enough information. Through this shared endeavor, we focus on what matters to teachers at each grade level, discover patterns that emerge, consider what is working well and what needs to be modified, and identify changes we need to make.

Many of the teachers I work with come to use running records on a regular basis in their classrooms. Teachers have moved beyond taking a running record twice a year during scheduled assessment times and now use running records to inform their instruction. Taking running records side by side with teachers helps me come to see the celebrations as well as any "glitches" they encounter. For each teacher, and each grade level, we explore how frequently children should be assessed. What do we learn when we take running records? We also examine how teachers choose praise points and teaching points. Then, we note how teachers record the praise points and teaching points. Next, we put a series of running records side by side to look for patterns for individual children, and then for patterns across the class. As teachers become more confident and competent at using running records, teachers see the value of the records as an ongoing assessment practice.

Once we have administered the assessments, I also work with teachers to score and interpret them. We analyze, score, and discuss writing samples and responses to literature. These conversations are informative and insightful—and can sometimes get quite heated. The back and forth, the push and pull, the tugs, and the nudges help us clarify what matters and what we want to assess.

In one district, after numerous heated conversations, I asked the teachers how they felt about an assessment that had been in place for several years. The teachers shared, "We've been using these end-of-the-book tests for years, and even though we designed them, they don't give us much information. Can we change it?" Assessing together started the process of inquiry. The difficult issues we grappled with were instructive and ultimately led to new assessments and new assessment procedures. Over the next few years, we put assessments into place that the teachers thought better reflected their teaching and student learning. The earlier difficult conversations led to transformative practices.

Understanding Formal Assessments

Just as teachers engage in literacy events as readers and writers (see Chapter 1), I ask them to take the state assessments their students are expected to complete. I also assign district- or school-level writing tasks so teachers and administrators can understand what they are asking of students when they administer these assessments. In this way, the teachers experience the tests and all of their accompanying emotions. They navigate the language of the tests, the formats, and the time constraints. As learners, we are reminded that we, too, need to wait to hear the directions and follow all outlined procedures. Although the test scoring is private, I am always interested to see how different teachers share how well (or not) they performed. I know that I have been annoyed (and a bit embarrassed) when I have missed items on the test!

By taking formal assessments, we can examine our instructional practices and consider necessary changes. When we look at the results of the formal assessments, we should examine whether we are supporting students and preparing them for the tests. What do we learn from the tests? As we interpret and analyze them, we look for patterns. Where are the students' strengths? Where are they experiencing difficulties? What is missing in terms of instruction? What language is consistent with the testing? What is inconsistent?

In one district, as we analyzed the responses to the state assessment, the teachers noted that the children were struggling with vocabulary questions. This led to further inquiry on vocabulary. When testing data is shared with teachers, together we articulate what we learn from the results and identify how these understandings will inform our instruction.

REPRESENTING STUDENTS—REPORT CARDS

When we have talked about assessments, completed assessments side by side, and examined our students' progress, conversations inevitably turn to report cards. At that point, I ask teachers (or a committee of teachers) to consider if their report cards privilege the criteria they want or intend to privilege. How are students represented? What does the report card say about our theories of learning? Are the components of the report card consistent with what matters to teachers and administrators? Is the report card language aligned with standards? Aligned with instruction? To redesign report cards, we consider language choices, categories of literate behaviors, expectations across grade levels, and sustainability. As you might guess, the stakes are high, and conversations often become quite heated. In one district, it took more than two years of sustained conversations before we could agree on language for the report cards. Every conversation provided an opportunity to articulate and clarify how we wanted to represent growth and learning. Although we came to recognize that redesigning report cards would always be a work in progress, we wanted the revised language to hold up over time.

ASSESSING MATERIALS

As a coach, I want to support teachers as they critique materials, workbooks, supplies, and professional books (Vogt and Shearer 2003). One way I do this is to ask teachers to examine the materials they are using with students, assessing whether or not the materials used are appropriate for readers. For instance, if teachers are primarily using test preparation materials and the materials are too hard (Clay 1993, 2000), we examine the implications of that. Even though materials may be designed to help students prepare for high-stakes testing, a constant diet of frustration-level texts will not support students to become strategic.

I have also helped teachers examine the workbooks they are using with the question, What do these materials privilege? Together, we considered whether or not workbooks (or which ones) are necessary. In one district, teachers noticed that they were not using the workbooks entirely, because many pages were filled with rote exercises, unrelated to strategic reading and writing. These conversations led teachers to conclude that money previously spent on several unexamined workbooks could be better spent on leveled texts.

Book rooms (Fountas and Pinnell 1996) are another resource coaches and teachers can assess. Book rooms are intended to meet student needs by providing a range of leveled texts. To assess the efficacy of book rooms, we question, Are there enough books on each level? Do we need more culturally responsive texts? Are all genres represented? What materials will support our learners?

To start book rooms, I first ask teachers to take stock of the materials that are already available in their classrooms and the school. They can then place leveled books in a book room to share. As the book room is expanded, we can begin to look for gaps. Because some teachers prefer to keep all resources in their classrooms, I am mindful to request only books that have been purchased with school funds at first! In fact, in one building where the book room is now thriving, we recently laughed about how initially teachers wouldn't part with their books. This was my first experience helping teachers set up a book room, and initially they gave only their oldest, most dilapidated books. Teachers were afraid that they wouldn't ever see their books again. As they saw beautiful new leveled books purchased and placed in the book room, they started, little by little, to add titles from their classrooms. Now that routines are in place, there are two book rooms, and teachers can keep books for extensive amounts of time in their classrooms without worrying that students in other classrooms will be shortchanged. In another building, our initial budget was so tight that we had to carry the leveled readers in baskets from one classroom to another (we agreed to switch every other week) so the children could read from a range of leveled texts.

As I help teachers examine the materials and supplies that they are using and need, I am sure to keep current on what is available from a range of catalogs, publishers, and companies. In this way, I can make recommendations for purposeful purchases.

ASSESSING YOUR ROLE AS A COACH

As a coach, how will I know if I am making a difference? Lyons (2002) reminds us of the importance of reflecting on our coaching (just as we ask teachers to reflect on their teaching). Each time I meet with teachers, I collect data in my notebook. Just as I take notes during guided reading lessons and writing conferences with students, I write down teacher comments, insights, and questions raised during each interaction. I return to these notes when I meet with teachers. For instance, when a third-grade teacher shared during a meeting that she was planning to try a new system for tracking her writing conferences, I was sure to find out how it was going the next time we met. Another teacher wanted to extend her repertoire of prompts during guided reading. When I met her in the hallway, I asked how this was going, and whether she wanted or needed additional support. Taking copious notes, revisiting these notes, and highlighting them for future use helps inform future interactions with teachers and helps me know whether change is occurring. I cycle back to my notes to let the teachers know their voices matter and that I am following up on their self-initiated areas for change.

Just as I encourage teachers to do with students, I look for patterns with the teachers. Whereas some teachers work through or comment on the same issues repeatedly, others move to new areas for growth. This also lets me know which teachers are taking risks as learners. In looking through my notes, I can evaluate whether I am moving too quickly. For instance, I noticed that although most teachers were comfortable considering author's intent and asking children to explore multiple perspectives, the social-justice thread of critical literacy was taking longer to understand and embrace. From listening to conversations in classrooms and during our grade-level meetings, I learned we needed to engage in more professional readings and discussions together on critical literacy.

I look for ways teachers are taking risks as learners and transferring ideas, language, and practices from coaching interactions to their classrooms. Transfer is one form of evidence of teachers' developing self-extending systems (Dozier and Rutten 2005/2006). Instructional changes occur when teachers take ownership of their professional growth and student achievement. Lyons and Pinnell (2001) maintain, "Coaching expands teachers' conceptual knowledge in a way that helps them learn from their own teaching over time" (139). Quick fixes and prescriptions may lead to improved assessment data, but once the coach leaves, teachers may revert to unexamined practices.

I also look to see if administrators are stimulating and promoting a culture of inquiry in their buildings and districts. Teachers need time and opportunities for their practices to become rooted in their everyday teaching lives. Administrators can support these efforts, with the celebrations and difficulties that accompany inquiry. In Chapter 9, Peggy O'Shea and Micah Brown, two administrators in districts where I have done extensive coaching, talk about the changes they have noticed in their districts and buildings.

08 Frequently Asked Questions About Coaching

As you read this chapter, consider it the start to a conversation on practicalities, logistical considerations, and conceptual understandings. Some of the questions and answers center around establishing routines and procedures, whereas others are more conceptually oriented. There is a purposefulness behind everything a coach does. Some practices and procedures are readily put into place, and others will evolve from your work meeting the specific needs of the teachers with whom you engage. Within this chapter, I attempt to illustrate the parallel nature for these practicalities in your literacy coaching and in teachers' lives in their classrooms.

 When organizing a workshop or a meeting, what are some logistics and practicalities I need to consider?

Agendas

Whether I am working one on one, with a small group, or with a large group, I develop an agenda. In doing so, I become clear, focused, and deliberate in my planning. The agendas are intentional documents that also become teaching opportunities. In each agenda, I embed questions for consideration and ideas for the teachers to refer to in the future.

At the beginning of each meeting or session, I hand out the agenda to the teachers. We use this as a working document for our time together. Teachers are invited to add to the agenda throughout the time together and to set the table for future interactions—be it during future workshops, our classroom visits, or one-on-one conversations.

I reread previous agendas, take notes, highlight, and use the information to guide the development of the next session(s). I reflect on what the teachers have said and return to those points to extend future conversations. In this way, every session builds upon the previous session. For example, when teachers share that they are going to try out new practices, I am sure to ask how those are going. When teachers share that they plan to read professional books, I ask them if the particular book worked for them, and how so. If we have brainstormed several possibilities because a particular instructional practice was difficult, I want to be sure to learn if the suggestions were helpful, or if we need to brainstorm more possibilities.

When teachers see the benefits of the agendas, they often decide to use them in their classrooms. They say the specificity of the agendas lead them to use them as instructional vehicles, just as agendas are used during our sessions. They also say the agendas serve as a learning tool and a reference when I am not there. Agendas also provide a reflective space. "Oh, I'd forgotten about that," teachers say, or, "I used to try out... I'd gotten away from that."

Linda, a primary-level reading teacher, uses the agenda as a reflective space for her teaching. "I read the agendas to refresh my memory, to reflect on instructional practices," she says. "I ask myself, Has it become a part of my repertoire, or do I need to review it again? Right now, I feel comfortable with book introductions, so I won't need to review those. Now I'm looking at the time we talked about writer's craft. Are we reading like writers? I keep looking at the agendas to see if I'm leaving out pieces or if there are parts I've forgotten."

Transfer to Classrooms

In the literacy lab, teachers routinely use agendas with their students and talk about how these agendas readily transfer to their own classrooms outside one-on-one tutorials. When time is short, as it generally is, both in our time together in the lab and in classrooms, the agendas become spaces for negotiating what content will be covered and what will have to wait. Agendas easily transfer to classrooms and are a way to help students make instructional decisions for their learning. Prompts I've used include the following:

- *Because we have time for only one of the following [instructional practice], which should we do? Let's talk about that/vote on that…*

- *In what order do we want to try things out today?*

- *Where would you like to begin?*

Lists

I am a list maker. I make lists of materials I need to bring for every meeting and session. In these lists, I include overheads I plan to use, handouts, professional resource books, articles, highlighters, markers, and paper. When I have a short time to meet with an individual, I want to be sure I have the professional resource book I was planning to share or the copy of an article I have promised. Lists transfer to the classroom, too. Because I forget things easily, I ask children to write things down to remind me. I'll often say, "Make a list for me." Students can also see how lists help people organize for learning. As a writer, I make a list each evening to set a clear purpose for my work the next day. At the end of writer's workshop, give children the opportunity to stop, pause, and reflect where they want their work to go the next time they write. Generating lists can become a normal part of the learning routine.

Structuring Learning Groups

I am deliberate in how I structure groups during workshop sessions. Different group structures facilitate different types of learning opportunities. When participants work in pairs, the intimacy of the partnership often encourages teachers and learners to be more secure. Most important, in a pair, everyone has a voice. Many teachers are willing to take more risks in smaller groups. When teachers or learners are placed in groups of three or more, some can check out of the conversation. Some let one or two people do all the talking. It is important to provide opportunities for everyone to have a voice in the conversations. Assigning roles offers a way to structure learning initially. But even though this works to get conversations started, it is important to help teachers (and learners) move beyond the roles provided. If we choose to use roles extensively, it is also important to make sure that learners engage in the full range of those offered.

Working in groups places teachers (and learners) with others who will move them forward—in their thinking, their dialogue, their language. I am mindful to place teachers in a range of groups (across grade levels, across different types of learners) to avoid getting "stuck." In this way, teachers can see the range of ways others are thinking and engaging in tasks. Some coaches assign seating. I have done this rarely. I know I like to choose where I sit, and this influences my thinking.

Transfer to Classroom

Teachers have commented that they like the range of ways in which I organize groups (cards, numbering off, predetermined selections, alphabetically) and that they transfer the model(s) to their classrooms. I also articulate to the teachers how I structure groups. This leads them to consider the following: How do we structure our students to work together? Why does this matter? What are pitfalls to avoid in the classroom? We can notice challenges when we work together in groups as adults and then bring these understandings to our structuring of student groups in classrooms.

? *As you set up a meeting room, what do you do to create a learning space?*

When designing a meeting space, the choices I make are based on community building. If I'm meeting one on one, I want to create a private, invitational space. I look for comfortable chairs. Where can we sit together so there is no power differential? I look for places where we can easily sit side by side to talk together and to look at documents, artifacts, student writing, and work samples.

For larger groups, I look to see where I can most easily create a comfortable learning space. The first thing I do for group meetings is organize the environment so that we can all see one another and have enough room to write comfortably and share student work samples. I consider the following to ensure that everyone can be part of the conversation: Round tables invite collaboration. Long tables have to be placed to keep the space invitational so that distance is not created. What spaces do we need to share our artifacts? Mentor texts? What about our environment invites writing, collaboration, and learning?

Transfer to Classroom

Just as I work to create a learning space when working with teachers, I ask teachers to consider physical learning spaces when they are creating their classrooms. Do they prefer desks? Round tables? Long tables? How are learning centers organized and placed within the classroom? Is there an area for gathering together to look at the easel, the overhead projector, or the classroom library? Where are the areas that encourage sustained opportunities for collaboration? Where do students get to put their materials?

Names

I believe it is important that we all address each other by name. If some of the teachers are new to the building or district, I make sure to provide name cards and markers. It is interesting to see how people choose to represent themselves as they decorate their cards. For some, color matters. I've had teachers wait several minutes to get the color they wanted.

I also make a seating chart for myself for each session and am mindful to quickly learn the name of each teacher. Students notice when we learn their names as well. When I wander through the halls, I feel better when I address the children by name.

Food

Good things happen around food. Food invites sharing, collaboration, and a bringing together of community. From the chocolate on my desk at work, to the treats we organize for our time together, food matters.

What are some ways to end my sessions with teachers?

I like to end each interaction or session with the questions, What did you learn today? What are you thinking? What are you planning to do? Asking these questions each session (a predictable framework) guides teachers to notice. Teachers are given the space to step back and reflect on the question, What did I learn? They hear the different responses from their colleagues. Teachers are expected to participate and engage in the day's session or one-on-one interaction. Just as we expect children to learn, this is a space for teachers to actively engage in learning.

When teachers respond to this question, I write down what each one says, including my own response. The question names the teachers as learners. I then refer to these responses for planning purposes. Returning to the responses becomes a part of our connected conversation. It lets participants know that I am listening and am responsive to their learning, to their questions, and to their words. "Last time we met you shared that you were planning to try status of the class. How is that going?" The teachers' voices matter and are integral to our time together.

The following are responses to the questions, What did you learn today? What are you thinking about?

Denise: To consider the language I'm using in my classroom. Now I know I need to examine it. Before I said things out of habit.

Melanie: To try not to impose so much of who I am. I like to rush, rush, rush and run my classroom in the same way. I learned today that not everyone functions the same on my time frame. I've forgotten about those kids who like to sit back and think.

Linda: How to help the teaching assistants engage in instructional conversations. I like the idea of starting with the prompt, As you read, decide when…. As you read, consider how…. These will help students have more conversations and will give more ownership to the students and empower them as we send them back to the book. It's not so much imposing anymore; it is more open ended.

Carly: I'm going to problematize engagement. It's not so much a measure of who's engaged, but how are they engaged? We learn from those who don't engage to help us rethink engagement. And I loved Linda's question, How are they [the students] acting like an editor?

Another prompt I routinely use is, "What will you try in your classrooms?" The following responses were given after a session on the writing process:

> *"I'm going to be sure that I am clear about the purpose and audience when my students write."*
> *"I liked the Have-a-Go notebook. I'm going to try it."*
> *"I'm going to notice when my students have stamina."*

Transfer to Classroom

The question, What did you learn today? transfers readily to classrooms. Responses to this question provide a window into students' understanding. In my classroom, this was a student's ticket out the door at the end of each day. I ask this question every time I work with learners, from my kindergarten classroom to my doctoral classes. I want to model active participation and learning, so I want to engage in language that situates and names my students as learners. Asking, What did you learn today? brings the community together as we finish our work together for that day.

How do I help teachers organize and manage their literacy instruction?

This question immediately leads me to numerous questions. First, what time frame are teachers looking to manage? Are they trying to find time to incorporate all of their literacy instruction? Guided reading time? Writer's workshop time? How long are their literacy blocks? Do they currently have literacy blocks? After considering time frames, we move to what happens during those time frames. What are students doing as the teachers conduct their guided reading groups? How long do groups last? For instance, how much text are children reading daily? How much text are they writing daily? Are we supporting students to develop fluency and stamina? In what ways? In what ways are teachers engaging students? It is essential to explore a range of responses to these questions. Together, we develop models for literacy blocks. Teachers can then try these out, and we can revise as needed. It is always interesting to see how and when teachers organize their literacy blocks and what they consider valuable learning opportunities.

One hint for managing literacy centers: I routinely advise teachers to initially use timers during their guided reading sessions. Timers are helpful for the teachers until they recognize what twenty or thirty minutes together "feels" like. When the timer goes off, I ask the teachers to stop and analyze their time with students. Questions we consider: How was my book introduction? Too long? Too short? Did my students have enough time for sustained reading? Where could I extend? Where could I cut back? What about our discussion? Did it feel too long? Too short? Teachers in one district, as I was modeling a guided reading lesson, cut me off mid-word when the timer rang—just as I had recommended they do. After this reflection, we can consider if the time frame is workable and ways we can make our instructional time even more valuable.

How do I help teachers reconsider and rework their schedules?

Time on task has received renewed attention. Former IRA president Richard Allington (2005) asked teachers to look for ways to increase instructional time. To examine schedules, I ask teachers to document their teaching time for an entire week. All minutes are considered in this exercise. Then, I open the conversation with the following: "Examine the way your day is spent. See what it says about what you privilege as a teacher. Is it what you want to privilege? Where are your spaces to revisit? What spaces do you want to rethink?"

When teachers reflect on their schedules, they can begin to reenvision ways to increase instructional time. Many notice the multiple transition times and "down times" daily. This is an important start to the conversation. We look for ways to incorporate more instruction during transition times or to limit the transition times. As I help teachers reconsider their schedules, invariably they find "spaces" they are willing to consider, and spaces they are not willing to change. I am mindful of this as I help them recreate their scheduling. Two specific areas I often address when discussing schedules are calendar time and transition time.

Calendar Time

Why do we have calendar time every day from the time children are in day care through second or third grade? What are the benefits? What are the trade-offs? There are benefits, but there are also instructional trade-offs when calendar time becomes an established twenty- to thirty-minute daily routine over numerous years (180 days times 4–6 years). I ask teachers to consider what is left out of our instruction if this practice is not examined. When examined mathematically, the numbers are staggering. Multiply 180 days by 20 minutes and you get 3,600 minutes. That 3,600 minutes times 4 years

(K, 1, 2, 3) equals 14,400 minutes. That would be sixty hours per year on calendar and 240 hours over four years. After exploring this, we might decide that indeed calendar matters for those numbers, but should it remain an unexamined practice?

Transitions

I do the same for transition time. Arguably, transitions are a necessary part of classroom life. But, consider the following transition schedule: ten minutes to line up for lunch, five minutes to transition from class to class, ten minutes after lunch recess, ten minutes to pack up for home. That becomes 35 minutes times 180 days, which equals 6,300 minutes per year: 105 hours per year on transitions. These numbers are sobering, and coaches can help teachers examine their schedules for places to think anew and ways to bring literacy to the forefront.

How can we make transitions become more meaningful? For instance, as you line up students, why not ask them to tell you the best word they've heard or written all morning or all afternoon? These transitions could be used to extend vocabulary development and help students see that words are intriguing and interesting—everywhere, not just during a lesson. Such transitions encourage students to transfer their learning from one space to another. The point of this exercise is to put established routines and practices on the table for critical examination.

Administrative Support

After I meet with teachers to discuss scheduling, we bring in the principal to help consider and secure scheduling. Some suggestions to consider are having similar prep times and/or similar lunchtimes for planning purposes, having specials in the afternoon for primary grades so they have large literacy blocks in the morning, having schoolwide sustained silent reading time, and being mindful when children are pulled for special services and for activities such as band, chorus, and music lessons. All of these issues influence our instructional time together.

When do I schedule time to work together with people?

As I work with teachers, I am guided by Brian Cambourne's advice: "Go with the goers." Start your work with those who are interested in collaborative relationships and rethinking their instructional practices. Visit their classrooms, try out instructional practices in their rooms, become a part of the landscape of their rooms. These teachers will become your best advocates. Once people hear about the partnerships you are developing with other teachers, they will become more interested and involved. I remember hearing from one teacher early on, "I think I'll just toe in…. I know my friend wants to dive in and make all these changes, but putting my toe in the water is just enough for me." I appreciated her candor and was mindful to check on her comfort level as we worked together.

How do I go about organizing professional development libraries and recommending books, articles, and resources to teachers?

Choosing texts for our children matters. Recommending professional books for our teachers matters. As coaches, we want to consider which professional books will be the most welcoming for our teachers as learners and where we can guide them next. Sometimes, teachers want books that contain practical advice, whereas other times they prefer books that are more conceptual. With teachers' busy lives, this might be the only professional development book they read for the year (or one of a few), so I want it to match teachers' needs and interests. Teachers trust you as a coach to set them on a productive path—you've read a wider range of research, articles and books, and you've attended more conferences. As I read through the research, I consider who would find particular articles and books interesting. As teachers support their students and nudge them forward in their literacy development, my job is to nudge teachers forward pedagogically and conceptually.

When districts are short of money, they want the most for their dollars. Initially, I recommended all professional books and resources for everyone in the building. I've come to believe that this is not the best use of resources. In fact, one text for the whole building could encourage teachers to use the same text for all students in their classrooms. We want teachers to consider a variety of texts for their students. As coaches, we set the example by providing teachers with an array of text choices. In turn, teachers can consider if their text selections are specific to their students' needs, wants, and interests. I have found that buying one book or resource per grade level or per building is an excellent way to begin developing a professional development library. When teachers show additional interest, we buy more copies. Buying fewer texts leads to shared conversations. We encourage the teachers to place Post-its in the books, to highlight sections they find interesting, and to recommend books to their colleagues. When teachers express an interest in study group texts, we purchase books for the study groups, with an extra or two for those who become interested after hearing the conversations.

How do I use my librarian as a resource?

Librarians are an invaluable resource for literacy coaches. In one library, the librarian coded books in the library as mentor texts—books with great leads, books with powerful language, and so on, providing books for read-alouds, new series, and new authors. Librarians are also resources for inquiry projects, technology, Internet resources, and genre studies. In many schools, professional development books are housed in the library.

Librarian Mindy Grey offered the following: "By nature we want to help and share. We offer interlibrary loan if we don't have what you are looking for; give both structured and impromptu book talks, including new books, books on particular subjects, etc; run book clubs for students and adults; put together webquests and playlists on United Streaming; collect and organize recommended sites for both teachers and students. We *love* suggestions for purchase since we have lots of vendor contacts and can sometimes get preview or freebie materials."

As a coach, how do I extend my literacy content knowledge?

Much has been written about the importance of the literacy coach as an intellectual leader. To become a literacy leader, look for ways to extend your knowledge of the field of literacy. Read widely to learn about instructional practices, current research, and available resources for teachers and students. Stay current. You will want to know the theory to inform your practice. Read, read, read—research journals, professional journals, professional books, and Web sites. Attend conferences—local conferences, statewide conferences, and national conferences. Find other coaches (in or out of your district/school/context) to share ideas, stories, and wonderings. Join your local IRA affiliates and NCTE affiliates.

After you have dipped into the literature, find your entry point. Reflect. Become strategic. Where are your strengths? Set a course of action. How will you spend your time? Will you focus primarily on writing this year or this part of the year? Will you concentrate on reading instruction at this point? When you attend conferences, focus on one or two particular areas or strands. Ask your teachers what areas they would like you to bring back information from. Last year, as I was heading to NCTE, the teachers in one of the buildings I was working in wanted to learn more about conferring. I attended sessions on conferring and brought back handouts to weave into our discussions and lessons. Also, find one or two sessions that are for sheer fun or that are completely different than any session you tried earlier. Consider, what do you want the sessions to do for you?

Take notes on the books you read. As you read, think about which teachers would benefit from certain chapters, articles, and books based upon their interests. Read extensively to know which resources to recommend to your teachers. Strategically place articles in mailboxes. Send links to Web sites to your teachers.

Read children's literature. Get teachers hooked on new books. Just as we want teachers to read widely to know which books to recommend to their students, you want to know as a literacy leader which resources to recommend to your teachers.

As a literacy coach, how do I improve, extend, or refine my instructional practices?

First, find classrooms of teachers you trust at multiple grade levels. In these classrooms, try out the instructional practices you recommend as a coach. I'm always trying new instructional practices and learning from children. In these classes, I can address issues of timing, transitions, and logistics when implementing new practices. In every classroom, I experiment, grow, and learn with the teachers and children. These classrooms and teachers became trusted learning spaces for me.

By working side by side with teachers and students, I better understand the expectations and student competencies at a range of grade levels. Multiple classrooms at multiple grade levels widen the lens on teaching and learning. In turn, this helps me address and understand specific concerns and questions raised as teachers (and I) begin to try new practices. I've learned that when I teach students in classrooms, I grow as a teacher of students as well as a teacher of teachers.

As a coach, I gain credibility when teachers recognize that I have actually engaged in the practices I am recommending. I am sure to model how I introduced the lesson and share my problem-solving throughout. In working through the glitches—and describing how I worked through them— teachers have shared that they appreciate my candor in openly discussing any issues or difficulties I encountered while implementing new practices.

Once I am routinely in classrooms and have established a trusting relationship, I collect student work samples to use for illustrative purposes. I always secure permission from parents and students (making sure that students remain anonymous). I use these work samples in multiple ways. For example, what actually happened when I taught the lesson? What competencies are evident? What do I learn across time? What did I learn across assignments? What did I learn about the directions I gave?

How am I positioned in my role as a coach?

How we are labeled in many ways frames our identities. This is true for coaches, for teachers, and for students. Language choices matter. Are you perceived as an expert? Knowledgeable other? Support? Advocate? Trainer? Co-learner? Several of the above? Is this the role you want? How are you positioning yourself? How are others positioning you (intentionally or unintentionally)? How are people approaching you? Step back and look for patterns. How people approach me lets me know how they see my role. Is this the role I envisioned? Is there another way I would like people to see me, respond to me, or interact with me? What can I learn about my role or extending my role as I examine these patterns?

I work hard to be known as someone who works collaboratively, someone who builds partnerships and trusting relationships. I prefer to be seen as a co-learner, an advocate, a knowledgeable other rather than as a trainer or an expert. I am uncomfortable when I hear, "You're the expert. Tell us what to do." Or "You're the trainer. You're supposed to know." Others may choose and be very comfortable in a training capacity. It depends on how you envision your role, and how others envision your role. As a coach, how do you name yourself? How do others name you? After examining this, consider whether this is how you want to be named.

 I have novice teachers and veteran teachers in the same group/at the same grade level. What do I do?

When I'm working with children, it is my job to consider the learners' zones of proximal development. It is the same when I work with teachers. Learning from one another is generative. First, I work to identify and build on each teacher's strengths. New teachers bring fresh ideas to the table, and veterans bring years of experience and understanding of logistics. I also create learning opportunities for all teachers to inquire collaboratively. It is exciting when novice teachers share ideas and veteran teachers embrace or tentatively try out a new idea. In one grade-level meeting, a kindergarten teacher shared the family journals she was sending home with her students. Later, during break, I heard her describe to several veteran teachers how she was using the journals to link home and school literacies.

I've been asked to evaluate the teachers in my building. Won't this damage my role as a coach?

A coach's role is to advocate, not evaluate. As a coach you want to be clear to all participants that your job is not to evaluate teachers, but rather to provide assistance as they reconsider and refine instructional practices. To develop a trusting relationship, it is imperative that teachers be willing to seek advice and support from you. Here is where you and the administrators you work with need to "protect" your role as an advocate, not an evaluator. This is, indeed, a delicate balance and will most likely require routine conversations with administrators to ensure that you are not asked to evaluate the very colleagues who have trusted you to help them improve their teaching. It is not your job to take teachers' vulnerabilities and expose them to the administration.

What happens if one group of teachers is strong and another grade level is not?

Mix up the groups! When teachers work with teachers at other grade levels, they can see instructional practices, curriculum markers, and testing concerns from the range of grade levels present. Mixing up the groups also helps teachers see the range of expectations and responsibilities as well as which areas of the curriculum are stressed in the different grades. Most important, engaging conversations ensue about how students take up the curriculum in a variety of settings. Teachers often have conversations about former students and can see or hear about student progress and growth over time. These conversations help teachers "step outside the box" of their own grade level.

In addition to learning about other grade-level curriculum concerns and instructional practices, it mixes up personalities. Just recently I heard from a primary teacher,

"How refreshing it was to work with the fifth-grade teachers. I rarely see them in my building. I had no idea what a great sense of humor they had."

 What happens if ideologically I disagree with the practices of the programs or procedures I'm expected to implement and promote?

Here are some questions to consider if you believe you are in this position: Are you in the right building? The right district? Are your talents as a coach being used or thwarted at every turn? Is it worth battling on a daily basis? Is there another building or another district that is more consistent with your literacy vision?

When students graduate from our master's degree program, we caution them that they are interviewing as well as being interviewed during their job searches and to consider compatibility. This can be a difficult lesson when they feel the pressure to be hired, especially in areas where teaching positions are difficult to secure. So, too, with coaching. If the programs you are or would be in charge of implementing are philosophically incompatible, you need to think long and hard about whether this is the right position for you.

 How can we move beyond "Not my kids...," "Yes, but...," and "Our schedule won't allow us to..."?

We can all note places in our lives where change comes more easily or readily for us and other places where we draw our line in the sand, and say, "No!" "Not now," or "Not yet." As coaches, we want to learn from our learners. When teachers (or students) choose not to engage, it is never easy. However, just as in classrooms, I can learn the most from teachers (and students) who are challenging. What can I learn about my approach, my style, my knowledge of literacy and literate processes from those who do not readily embrace change or working with me?

The first thing I try to do is to determine why an individual chooses not to engage. Has she had difficult experiences earlier? Is she cautious? Why? Does she have a prior history with coaches? I find an opportunity to talk one on one with the individual to discern the reason(s) for reluctance in engaging. My first response is to say, "I notice how quiet you are during our time together/at grade-level meetings/in workshops/when I visit. Tell me about this. Is there something I should know?" I am clear that I am there to support her learning and engagement with new instructional practices.

In attempting to discern why students choose not to engage, we consider the following: Is the task too difficult? Too easy? Are the directions clear enough? Is the book too easy? Too hard? We look for answers in our instructional practices, our language, our approaches, and the histories of the learners. I also work to find common interests and then frame our conversations around them. These experiences give us a sense of connectedness and provide a way for us to learn together.

There is no doubt that you will have many more questions as you coach. Although this chapter provides a starting point, the many participants in your coaching world will help you find answers, and in doing so, will generate more questions.

09 Sustaining Change Over Time

I am intrigued by how people make sense of their worlds.
This intrigue led me to become a teacher. As a classroom
teacher I was fascinated with how my students learned.
My elementary school classrooms were filled with inquiry
and conversations. My students questioned, wondered,
deliberated, debated, and constructed understandings
through conversations—the very conversations and inquiry
I seek to foster as a coach. As Tharp and Gallimore (1988)
note, "The instructional conversation can only occur
in a community of learners, and it is by means of that
conversation that the community is created" (34). Responsive
literacy coaching is about learning—learning together,
collaborating with colleagues, reflecting, and creating spaces
for inquiry. My goal is to create a community to explore
improving instructional practices for increased student
achievement.

To develop instructional relationships, I extend invitations
for learning and knowing, engage in inquiry through joint

productive activities, focus on the strengths of learners, consider and examine my language choices, and guide teachers as they build self-extending systems. The range of tools offered in this book invite customizing based upon a reader's particular instructional context. That the tools are not scripted is deliberate and invites movement within and among the tools. As coaches and teachers, we want a repertoire of instructional possibilities to draw from and a repertoire of tools to engage with in our coaching and teaching. Every day will include successful teaching moments, choices and decisions that we might change, or lessons we wished we had done differently. Engaging in reflection fosters an examination and a reexamination of literacy, teaching, and learning. This flexibility encourages moving beyond a "training" vision for teachers. Teacher professionalism and problem-solving are at the forefront, rather than simply following prescriptive lessons. As Fullan maintained during an interview with Dennis Sparks (2003), "We need far more intensive professional learning within a culture of continuous deliberation" (55). Together, we explore, What do our instructional choices privilege (intentionally or unintentionally)? What do our choices mean for our learners?

I am clear when I am working with teachers that although I will not necessarily have the answer (emphasizing that generally there isn't one "right" answer), I will help them explore and find possible solutions to their questions. As a co-learner (Cambourne 1995) rather than an expert, I learn from children, teachers, families, administrators, and instructional contexts. However, as a coach it is also critical to acknowledge and draw upon my areas of expertise. In doing so, I create opportunities for teachers to take on agentive stances, to build on their self-extending systems, and then support sustainability of their practices.

Fullan's emphasis on continuous deliberation necessitates a long-term commitment to teachers' growth and professional development. It helps us move beyond the thinking that everyone has had professional development in literacy. Literacy is done. Now we're moving to math or science. Continuous inquiry leads to substantive rather than superficial changes, but we need to remain mindful that change occurs at different times, in different ways, for different people. Teachers, like students, move on different paths as learners. Even when they are introduced to the same language, take part in modeled lessons, or participate in joint productive activities, each teacher experiences a coaching interaction in his or her own way. Teachers need scaffolding, time, and opportunities to engage in instructional practices and then transfer and extend their repertoire of instructional possibilities. As Purcell-Gates (1995) reminds us, "We are able to learn only what we can experience" (41). As we engage in collaborative inquiry, our conversations change over time.

Initially, teachers tend to adopt my language or the routines I use during modeled lessons. Early conversations are filled with teachers asking, "Am I doing it right?" With practice, teachers begin to adapt routines, practices, and procedures to fit their style of teaching and to meet the needs of the learners in their classrooms. This is when I routinely hear, "What is my nudge? Now I look forward to the nudge." Those conversations are not part of our initial discourse. As teachers become more confident and competent in their instructional practices, the coach's role shifts again. At this time, support becomes more fine-tuning of instructional practices—a "checking in," so to speak. This is also when teachers consider ideas and then create their own visions for instruction in their classrooms. When we have sustained time together, we can allow for the stops and starts that accompany learning.

EXPLORING POSSIBILITIES

The moment we start asking people to rethink or change their current instructional practices, we have to recognize that we may be asking them to move beyond their comfort zones. In virtually every situation, I am not the first (or only) person advocating for educational changes. Buildings have histories, teachers have histories, districts have histories, and bandwagons have come and gone. When I am working with teachers, I work to keep this at the forefront of my thinking. When we ask people to change, we have to consider *why* we are asking them to make changes and highlight how engaging in the change process benefits them. As a coach, I frame my recommendations as possibilities, rather than as absolutes. I want to encourage a community of inquiry, rather than a community where some teachers are positioned as knowers and "right," and others feel left out and silenced. If I am not mindful of this dynamic, I can promote defensiveness—and that's a problem. It becomes much harder to inquire, explore, rethink, and reconsider together, just as in classrooms. If some students are positioned as "stars" and knowers, and changers and movers, what does it do to the other learners?

SCHOOL CULTURE: THE EFFECT OF RESPONSIVE LITERACY COACHING

Throughout the book, I have focused primarily on how responsive literacy coaching has influenced teachers. Next, I consider how responsive literacy coaching has shaped the school culture in two educational contexts. Here, coaching over time will be explored through two administrators' eyes. Micah Brown is a principal in a K–2, Title 1 rural/suburban school with 410 students. In Micah's building, I initially worked with teachers to implement guided reading. Later, we focused on writing instruction and examined ways to connect and extend reading and writing instruction. Peggy O'Shea is an assistant superintendent in a small city school district with three K–5 elementary buildings, with a total of 917 students. Similarly, in Peggy's district, I initially worked to help teachers implement guided reading and later focused on writing instruction. Because elementary students frequently moved from one part of the district to another, we also worked to bring the literacy instruction of the elementary buildings into closer alignment.

Both administrators commented on their teachers' increasing level of professionalism. Teachers became more focused on the strengths and instructional needs of their learners. Teachers also increased their levels of specificity when discussing pedagogy and their students' literacy development. Although initial conversations focused more on the "right" way of implementing instructional practices, teacher conversations now center on multiple possibilities for engaging in practices.

CHANGES IN TEACHERS' INSTRUCTION

In discussing changes over time in teachers' instruction in her K–2 building, Micah focuses on collaborative partnerships, teachers' precision and increased attention to language, lesson development focused on the strengths and needs of the learner, and increased engagement of teachers and students.

> *Teachers are much more comfortable sharing ideas with one another, discussing together. Their classrooms are more open in that they invite each other in to observe and I arrange for the coverage. I've also noticed there is a much higher focus on language. The teachers are naming their instruction and are being more precise with language. The teachers think about lessons on two levels. They have gotten away from activity-based instruction to instruction that focuses on the needs for the students. The teachers are always thinking about the purpose of lessons. That turns into increased student interest, engagement, and joy! The teachers and students are still learning at the end of the year. There is much more time on task. Even*

*though there are only a few days left in the school year,
school is still going. It's the same thing at Christmas
and around the major breaks. They're always keeping
school alive!*

Micah also notes a difference in the conversations with
teachers taking a more agentive role for meeting student
needs. She comments that deficit-driven conversations are
waning, with teachers instead focusing first on the strengths
of the learner.

> *There has been a definite shift in that we definitely
> have discussions about instruction instead of blaming
> the learner. We're moving away from the "the family
> doesn't have," or "the family doesn't do" conversations.
> During meetings with pupil services we brainstorm
> instructional strategies versus spending half an hour
> discussing the deficiencies of parents. We've moved
> beyond deficiencies. Deficiencies can become endless
> if you get sucked down that path. We work from
> the strengths. What we do here does count for the
> kids—it does work. If a kid comes in with a paucity
> of vocabulary words, we need to work twice as hard
> to increase vocabulary. We can't judge socially. Our
> responsibility is to give the children more. We have
> high expectations and know our learners. At first the
> teachers were "doing" guided reading and "doing"
> writer's workshop. Now they're doing what is right for
> the learner.*

Peggy notes that the teachers in her district are
paying more attention to comprehension instruction and
conversations around texts. As a former reading teacher,
principal, and now assistant superintendent in her district,
Peggy can trace her teachers' evolution to increased
conversations about learners and a shared language
among them.

I've noticed that the teachers provide more in-depth instruction in comprehension. They now engage in conversations during reading, which fosters more interaction on the part of children. The teachers and students are making more connections when they read—text-to-text, text-to-life, text-to-author connections. When I first started as principal, people were still doing round-robin reading, and that's gone away. There is much more writing happening in the district. Literacy instruction is in full bloom at the kindergarten level, too. I've also noticed that there is a more gradual release of responsibility to the learner. As we've worked together, there is a shared language among the staff, and this translates to the students as well. We have more conversations around the learner at grade-level meetings and faculty meetings.

Peggy also focuses on shifts in assessment policies and practices. Over time, the conversations focused more centrally on the children as learners, and less about right and wrong procedures and policies.

In terms of assessment, although we still have to do the dotting the i's and crossing of the t's as we work through some of our assessment practices, there has been a loosening up, a shift in what our discussions look and sound like over the past four years. Now it is less about right and wrong. The teachers are focusing on the learners. There is more risk-taking on the part of the teachers, which leads to more risk-taking on the part of the students, which is how you learn.

CHANGES IN LEARNERS

Micah details the changes she noticed in her students as engaged readers and writers. She notes that children view writing as pleasurable and a way to transform policies in their community.

Children are talking about books more. Students are walking off the bus reading books. I've even had to tell some to stop and look ahead because it was a safety issue.

Writing has exploded. The level of student engagement is high. When you walk in a classroom, you can feel the concentration and engagement; it is palpable. There is much more writing displayed on the walls. The children are writing for purpose and are eager to take on challenges. They're writing to communicate, writing for joy and pleasure, using their imaginations. They've written to the president, to soldiers in Iraq, thank-you notes. Our Owl Post mailbox system started as a short-term Parents as Reading Partners (PARP) project, and teachers voted to continue it since the students were so excited to write letters to one another. They can send letters to siblings and friends at the intermediate school, too.

Students love sharing favorite books with me. There are increasing numbers coming into my office to share writing with me, and they're writing me more notes. Nancy's class changed the policy at the local library. Children are writing to the local paper, and some of their essays were recently published.

Peggy noted that students in her district were reading a wider range of genres and engaging in more purposeful reading and writing. She also focused on the children's strategic knowing. As children draw from their repertoire of strategies, they have come to name them as well.

I've noticed that children are reading more books across a variety of genres. They're excited about their reading, and they're more aware of what reading is all about. The reading and writing that they're doing is more purposeful and thoughtful. There are more conversations, and children are sharing more during discussions. This is transferring from the teachers, too. The children are using more strategies and are using language for their strategies. They're excited and telling us when they self-corrected. There are also more celebratory spaces. Children are reading their writing to invited guests.

SUSTAINING CHANGE OVER TIME

Micah outlined the ways she plans to sustain change over time. She focused on advocating for ongoing professional development and engaging in collaborative inquiry around student artifacts.

I'll continue to advocate for ongoing professional development. I want to continue to provide professional books, too. I've started to notice that if I can't buy it [a book] through the school, the teachers are buying the books on their own. I've been collecting a range of artifacts from the classroom, and we are becoming much more data based. I'm looking at monthly writing samples using the writing expectations we developed. In doing so, I can learn how the teachers think. If I think differently about the scoring, the teachers and I can talk about the writing pieces. I see certain things from a single piece of writing, while the teachers see their writers over time in the classroom. Reading the writing samples also helps me to get to know the children. I read all the writing in the hallway so I can talk to teachers and children about those pieces. I will continue scheduling sustained times for literacy [blocks] despite the difficulties that this scheduling entails.

Like Micah, Peggy focused on teacher collaborations. She pointed to encouraging a shared language and offering professional development based on teachers' needs.

> *To sustain teacher change, I want to continue to develop teacher collaboration. One teacher is currently running a study group, and now we have other teachers who want to start study groups. I want to keep the conversations ongoing so we have a common language. I'll continue to provide professional development based on the teachers' needs. For some, it is fine-tuning and keeping them up to date. I also have to look at funding allocations for professional development. Purchasing books is ongoing as we find new books to read and discuss. I want to keep a focus on our vision for literacy instruction and development and make sure new teachers have professional development opportunities as well. One thing I need to do is to bring the principals in even more. Everything is a work in progress. It is never completed.*

I see the ending of this book as filled with new beginnings. As Peggy says, everything is a work in progress. Each time I write, I come to learn what I know at a particular moment in time. Every time I enter a classroom, I learn anew. Each teaching and coaching moment offers multiple possibilities for exploration. As coaches and teachers we have opportunities to rewrite our histories, revising and reconsidering literacy and literacy development to deepen our knowledge and broaden our understandings.

The principles behind the tools outlined in this book insist that literacy coaches and teachers place the learner at the forefront of the learning enterprise, rather than the learner's skills. In this way, we help to move the learner forward. By creating classrooms where teachers attend to strengths first, we can avoid the trap of deficit-driven theorizing. Likewise, our goal as responsive literacy coaches is to attend to teachers' strengths first. As our relationships evolve and we engender trust, we can locate spaces where teachers are willing to reconsider instructional practices.

Responsive literacy coaching is generative. In responsive spaces, questioning leads to theorizing. Collaborating leads to partnerships. Inquiry leads to inquiring. Trusting leads to engendering trusting relationships. Risks lead to risk-taking. Examining leads to thoughtful examination. Analyzing leads to deeper analysis. Strengths lead to a strengths focus. Learning leads to sustained learning. Transfer leads to new understandings and competencies. And all lead to developing self-extending systems.

As a teacher, a researcher, and a coach I continue to grapple with the questions, What literacy environments and experiences are we creating for our teachers? What literacy environments and experiences are we creating in our schools for our students? Micah offers, "I want students to know that eventually you can change the world. When you contribute through reading and writing, our society grows. I want students to see themselves as scientists, mathematicians, poets, readers, writers." This is a good place to start.

A Appendix A:
Analysis of Writing Samples

Analysis of Writing Samples

SAMPLE 1	SAMPLE 2	SAMPLE 3
Topic:	Topic:	Topic:
Choice On Demand	Choice On Demand	Choice On Demand
Strengths of writer/content	Strengths of writer/content	Strengths of writer/content
Examples of interesting language	Examples of interesting language	Examples of interesting language
Evidence of revision	Evidence of revision	Evidence of revision
Evidence of editing	Evidence of editing	Evidence of editing
Conventions used (i.e., capitalization, punctuation, spelling, grammar)	Conventions used (i.e., capitalization, punctuation, spelling, grammar)	Conventions used (i.e., capitalization, punctuation, spelling, grammar)
Needs: Content	Needs: Content	Needs: Content
Conventions	Conventions	Conventions
Identify three (+) mini-lessons and/or mentor texts that will help move the writer forward. 1. 2. 3.	Identify three (+) mini-lessons and/or mentor texts that will help move the writer forward. 1. 2. 3.	Identify three (+) mini-lessons and/or mentor texts that will help move the writer forward. 1. 2. 3.
Other noticings:	Other noticings:	Other noticings:

B

Appendix B:
Guided Reading Observation
Forms for Learners and Teachers

Guided Reading Observation Form—Learner _____ Author _____ _____Guided Reading Level _____

Title of Text _____

NOTICINGS/STRENGTHS

	Student Language/Engagement

Book Introduction
 	
Predictions
 	
Connections made with the text
(t-a, t-s, t-t, t-I, t- w). When?
 	
In what ways does the child
attend to vocabulary?
 	
What behaviors do you notice
about the child's word-solving
strategies?
· Self-corrections
· What cueing systems does the
  child attend to? Ignore? –M, S, V
· Repetition
· Independence vs. appeals
· Use of illustrations
 	
Monitoring
Understanding
 	
Stamina
Multiple perspectives
Author's intent
Questioning the author
Social issues
 	
Attends to craft features
Attends to text features
	Behaviors:
	· Fluency/phrasing/
	  attention to punctuation
	· Finger pointing–when?
	· Voice print match
	· Book handling/
	  orientation
	· Directionality
	
	Level of engagement:
	Instructional conversations
	
	Discussions
	
	Think-alouds
	
	Constructs meaning
	
	Responses/reactions
	to text
	
	Sharing responses/
	reactions to text
	
	Surprises
	
	Other noticings:

Guided Reading Observation Form—Teacher

Title of Text _____ Author _____ Guided Reading Level _____

NOTICINGS/STRENGTHS		
How the teacher supports the learners:	Level of engagement. How are learners engaged?	Teacher Language
Book introduction	Instructional conversations	
Predictions	Discussions	
Goals/setting purpose		
Making connections to text	Think-alouds	
Attending to craft features	Constructing meaning	
Attending to text features		
Vocabulary development/ Introducing vocabulary Words	Response/reactions to text	
	Sharing responses/ reactions	
Reading behaviors noticed and named		
Monitoring understanding	Surprises	
Stamina		
Multiple perspectives	Other noticings:	
Author's intent		
Questioning the author		
Social issues		Ideas to Consider:

Professional References

Allington, R. 2002. *Big Brother and the National Reading Curriculum: How Ideology Trumped Evidence*. Portsmouth, NH: Heinemann.

———. 2005. "Urgency and Instructional Time." *Reading Today* 23 (1):17.

Allington, R. L., and S. Walmsley, eds. 1995. *No Quick Fix: Rethinking Literacy Programs in America's Elementary Schools*. New York: Teachers College Press.

Anders, P. L., J. V. Hoffman, and G. G. Duffy. 2000. "Teaching Teachers to Teach Reading: Paradigm Shifts, Persistent Problems, and Challenges." In M. L. Kamil, P. B. Mosenthal, P. D. Pearson, and R. Barr, eds. *Handbook of Reading Research* 3: 719–742.

Atwell, N. 1998. *In the Middle: New Understanding About Writing, Reading, and Learning*. 2d ed. Portsmouth, NH: Heinemann.

Bransford, J. D., and D. L. Schwartz. 1999. "Rethinking Transfer: A Simple Proposal with Multiple Implications." In A. Iran-Nejad and P. D. Pearson, eds., *Review of Research in Education* 24: 61–100. Washington, DC: American Educational Research Association.

Calkins, L. 2003. *Units of Study for Primary Writing: A Yearlong Curriculum, Grades K–2*. Portsmouth, NH: Heinemann.

Cambourne, B. 1995. "Toward an Educationally Relevant Theory of Literacy Learning: Twenty Years of Inquiry." *The Reading Teacher* 493:182–190.

Clark, C. M. 2001. "Good Conversation." In *Talking Shop: Authentic Conversation and Teacher Learning*, ed. C. M. Clark. New York: Teachers College Press.

Clay, M. M. 1991. *Becoming Literate: The Construction of Inner Control*. Portsmouth, NH: Heinemann.

———. 1993. *Reading Recovery: A Guidebook for Teachers in Training*. Portsmouth, NH: Heinemann.

———. 1998. *By Different Paths to Common Outcomes*. Portland, ME: Stenhouse.

———. 2000. *Running Records for Classroom Teachers*. Portsmouth, NH: Heinemann.

———. 2001. *Change Over Time in Children's Literacy Development*. Portsmouth, NH: Heinemann.

Cole, A., and J. G. Knowles. 2000. *Researching Teaching: Exploring Teacher Development Through Reflexive Inquiry*. Boston: Allyn and Bacon.

Commeyras, M. 2002. "Provocative Questions That Animate My Thinking About Teaching." *Language Arts* 80:129–133.

Compton-Lilly, C. 2003. *Reading Families: The Literate Lives of Urban Children*. New York: Teachers College Press.

Cook-Sather, A. 2001. "Translating Themselves: Becoming a Teacher Through Text and Talk." In *Talking Shop: Authentic Conversation and Teacher Learning*, ed. C. M. Clark. New York: Teachers College Press.

Darling-Hammond, L., and M. McLaughlin. 1996. "Policies That Support Professional Development in an Era of Reform."

In *Teacher Learning: New Policies, New Practices*, ed. M. McLaughlin and I. Oberman. New York: Teachers College Press.

Delpit, L. 2002. "No Kinda Sense." In *The Skin That We Speak: Thoughts on Language and Culture in the Classroom*, ed. L. Delpit and J. Kilgour Dowdy. New York: The New Press.

Dozier, C., 2001. *Constructing Teacher Knowledge: Learning from the Field*. Unpublished doctoral dissertation. University at Albany.

Dozier, C., P. Johnston, and R. Rogers. 2006. *Critical Literacy/Critical Teaching: Tools for Preparing Responsive Teachers*. New York: Teachers College Press.

Dozier, C. and I. Rutten. 2005/2006. "Responsive Teaching Toward Responsive Teachers: Mediating Transfer Through Intentionality, Enactment, and Articulation." *Journal of Literacy Research* 37(4):459–492.

Fletcher, R., and J. Portalupi. 1998. *Craft Lessons*. Portland, ME: Stenhouse.

Florio-Ruane, S., and T. Raphael. 2001. "Reading Lives: Learning About Culture and Literacy in Teacher Study Groups." In *Talking Shop: Authentic Conversation and Teacher Learning*, ed. C. M. Clark. New York: Teachers College Press.

Fountas, I., and G. Pinnell. 1996. *Guided Reading: Good First Teaching for All Children*. Portsmouth, NH: Heinemann.

Gallimore, R., and R. Tharp. 1990. "Teaching Mind in Society: Teaching, Schooling, and Literate Discourse." In *Vygotsky and Education: Instructional Implications and Applications of Sociohistorical Psychology*, ed. L. Moll. New York: Cambridge University Press.

Garnett, S. 2006. "Following the Lead: Connecting with Families Through Journals." In *Critical Literacy/Critical Teaching: Tools for Preparing Responsive Teachers*, ed. C. Dozier, P. Johnston, and R. Rogers. New York: Teachers College Press.

Goldenberg, C. 1992. "Instructional Conversations: Promoting Comprehension Through Discussion." *The Reading Teacher* 464:316–326.

Hawley, W., and L. Valli. 1999. "The Essentials of Effective Professional Development: A New Consensus." In *Teaching as the Learning Profession: Handbook of Policy and Practice*, ed. L. Darling-Hammond and G. Sykes. San Francisco: Jossey-Bass.

Hoffman, J. V., and P. D. Pearson. 2000. "Reading Teacher Education in the Next Millennium: What Your Grandmother's Teacher Didn't Know That Your Granddaughter's Teacher Should." *Reading Research Quarterly* 35:28–44.

International Reading Association. 2004. *The Role and Qualifications of the Reading Coach in the United States*. Newark, DE: International Reading Association.

———. 2006. *Standards for Middle and High School Literacy Coaches*. Newark, DE: International Reading Association.

John-Steiner, V., and T. Meehan. 2000. "Creativity and Collaboration in Knowledge Construction." In *Vygotskian Perspectives on Literacy Research*, ed. C. Lee and P. Smagorinsky. New York: Cambridge University Press.

Johnston, P. 1997. *Knowing Literacy: Constructive Literacy Assessment*. Portland, ME: Stenhouse.

———. 2004. *Choice Words: How Our Language Affects Children's Learning*. Portland, ME: Stenhouse.

Lave, J., and E. Wenger. 1991. *Situated Learning: Legitimate Peripheral Participation*. New York: Cambridge University Press.

Lyons, C. A. 2002. "Becoming an Effective Literacy Coach." In *Learning from Teaching in Literacy Education: New Perspectives on Professional Development*, ed. E. Rodgers and G. S. Pinnell. Portsmouth, NH: Heinemann.

Lyons, C. A., and G. S. Pinnell. 2001. *Systems for Change in Literacy Education*. Portsmouth, NH: Heinemann.

Lyons, C. A., G. S. Pinnell, and D. E. DeFord. 1993. *Partners in Learning: Teachers and Children in Reading Recovery*. New York: Teachers College Press.

McNaughton, S. 2002. *Meeting of Minds*. Wellington, New Zealand: Learning Media Limited.

Mercer, N. 2000. *Words & Minds: How We Use Language to Think Together*. New York: Routledge.

Moll, L., C. Amanti, D.Neff, and N. Gonzalez. 1992. "Funds of Knowledge for Teaching: Using a Qualitative Approach to Connect Homes and Classrooms." *Theory into Practice* 31:132–141.

Noddings, N. 1984. *Caring: A Feminine Approach to Ethics and Moral Education.* Berkeley: University of California Press.

———. 2005 "Caring in Education," *The Encyclopedia of Informal Education*, www.infed.org/biblio/noddings_caring_in_education.htm. August 16.

Orellana, M., and A. Hernandez. 1999. "Talking the Walk: Children Reading Urban Environmental Print." *The Reading Teacher* 52(6):612–619.

Purcell-Gates, V. 1995. *Other People's Words: The Cycle of Low Literacy.* Cambridge, MA: Harvard University Press.

Raider-Roth, M. 2005. *Trusting What You Know. The High Stakes of Classroom Relationships.* San Francisco, CA: Jossey-Bass.

Routman, R. 2005. *Writing Essentials: Raising Expectations and Results While Simplifying Teaching.* Portsmouth, NH: Heinemann.

Shockley, B., B. Michalove, and J. Allen. 1995. *Engaging Families: Connecting Home and School Literacy Communities.* Portsmouth, NH: Heinemann.

Sparks, D. 2003. "Change Agent: Interview with Michael Fullan." *Journal of Staff Development, 24 1*, 55–58.

Tannen, D. 2006. *You're Wearing That? Understanding Mothers and Daughters in Conversation.* New York: Random House.

Tharp, R., and R. Gallimore. 1988. *Rousing Minds to Life: Teaching, Learning, and Schooling in Social Context.* New York: Cambridge University Press.

Tharp, R., P. Estrada, S. Dalton, and L. Yamauchi. 2000. *Teaching Transformed: Achieving Excellence, Fairness, Inclusion, and Harmony.* Boulder, CO: Westview Press.

Toll, C. 2005. *The Literacy Coach's Survival Guide: Essential Questions and Practical Answers.* Normal, IL: International Reading Association.

Vinz, R. 1996. *Composing a Teaching Life.* Portsmouth, NH: Heinemann.

Vogt, M. E., and B. Shearer. 2003. *Reading Specialists in the Real World: A Sociocultural View*. Boston, MA: Allyn and Bacon.

Vygotsky, L. 1978. *Mind in Society: The Development of Higher Psychological Processes*. Cambridge, MA: Harvard University Press.

Walpole, S., and M. McKenna. 2004. *The Literacy Coach's Handbook: A Guide to Research Based Practice*. New York: Guilford Press.

Wells, G. 2000. "Dialogic Inquiry in Education: Building on the Legacy of Vygotsky." In *Vygotskian Perspectives on Literacy Research: Constructing Meaning Through Collaborative Inquiry*, ed. C. D. Lee and P. Smagorinsky. New York: Cambridge University Press.

Children's Literature Cited

Choldenko, Gennifer. 2004. *Al Capone Does My Shirts*. New York: Scholastic.

Dahl, Roald. 1961. *James and the Giant Peach*. New York: Puffin.

Finchler, Judy. 1996. *Miss Malarkey Doesn't Live in Room 10*. New York: Walker.

Frank, Anne. 1948. *Diary of a Young Girl*. New York: Bantam.

Gibbons, Gail. 1999. *The Pumpkin Book*. New York: Scholastic.

Golding, William. 1954. *Lord of the Flies*. New York: Penguin.

Hoff, Syd. 1958. *Danny and the Dinosaur*. New York: Harper Collins.

L'Engle, Madeline. 1962. *A Wrinkle in Time*. New York: Random House.

Lowry, Lois. 1989. *Number the Stars*. Boston: Houghton Mifflin.

Mayer, Mercer. 1998. *Just Me and My Puppy*. New York: Golden Books.

Nolen, Jerdine. *In My Momma's Kitchen*. New York: Harper Trophy.

Rayner, Shoo. 1989. *Victor Books*. A children's book series. Oxford, UK: Oxford University Press.

Reynolds, Peter. 2004. *ish*. Cambridge, MA: Candlewick.

Shannon, David. 2004. *Alice the Fairy*. New York: Scholastic.

Whitcomb, Mary. 1998. *Odd Velvet*. San Francisco: Raincoast Books.

WEBSITES

www.enchantedlearning.com

www.ira.org

www.ncte.org

www.windows.ucar.edu

www.worldbookonline.com

Index